# Decision Making

## TOWARDS AN EVOLUTIONARY
## PSYCHOLOGY OF RATIONALITY

# Decision Making

## TOWARDS AN EVOLUTIONARY
## PSYCHOLOGY OF RATIONALITY

Mauro Maldonato

Translated by
Jessica Vingerhoeds-Carbino

**sussex**
ACADEMIC
PRESS
*Brighton • Portland • Toronto*

2 4 6 8 10 9 7 5 3 1

*First published 2010 in Great Britain by*
SUSSEX ACADEMIC PRESS
PO Box 139
Eastbourne BN24 9BP

*and in the United States of America by*
SUSSEX ACADEMIC PRESS
920 NE 58th Ave        Suite 300
Portland, Oregon 97213–3786

*and in Canada by*
SUSSEX ACADEMIC PRESS (CANADA)
90 Arnold Avenue, Thornhill, Ontario L4J 1B5

*British Library Cataloguing in Publication Data*
A CIP catalogue record for this book is available from the British Library.


*Library of Congress Cataloging-in-Publication Data*
Maldonato, Mauro.
Decision making : towards an evolutionary psychology of rationality /
    Mauro Maldonato.
    p. ; cm.
Includes bibliographical references and index.
ISBN 978-1-84519-421-5 (p/b : alk. paper)
    1. Decision making. I. Title.
[DNLM: 1. Decision Making—physiology. 2. Adaptation, Psychological.
3. Cognitive Science. 4. Evolution. BF 448 M244d 2010]
BF448.M355 2010
153.8'3—dc22

                                                                                2010016822

The paper used in this book is certified by The Forest Stewardship Council (FSC), a non-profit international organization established to promote the responsible management of the world's forests. Products carrying the FSC label are independently certified to assure consumers that they come from forests that are managed to meet the social, economic and ecological needs of present and future generations.


Typeset and designed by Sussex Academic Press, Brighton & Eastbourne.
Printed by TJ International, Padstow, Cornwall.
This book is printed on acid-free paper.

# Contents

# Decision Making

## TOWARDS AN EVOLUTIONARY
## PSYCHOLOGY OF RATIONALITY

# An Evolutionary Hypothesis of Rationality

It is indeed astounding the number of decisions that humans have made from the beginnings of the species until the present day. For one and a half million years, driven by the restlessness that distinguishes them from all other living species, human beings have taken part in a great diaspora which first made them abandon the savannah and then urged them on to the conquest of the most remote and inhospitable corners of the planet: from the edges of deserts to the frozen tundra of the North. Each and every single decision was made by choosing among the possible alternatives in which the future manifested itself to them, often without any possibility of turning back. Moreover, as we are still here to reconstruct human history and analyse the countless decisions made throughout that long and complicated journey across the millennia, those decisions were adaptively successful.

Today we no longer face frequent life-or-death dilemmas, but the number of decisions that we are called upon to make is just as high as it was in the past. We are not even conscious of the majority of these decisions, while others require a great and conscious investment of time and energy. Without human beings' ability to choose, evolution would have been unthinkable or even inconceivable, and in any case it was certainly difficult, for humans had to adapt to the universe on the basis of incomplete, fragmentary information and above all starting with limited cognitive capacities and restricted time limits. In order to respond to the challenges of the environment, an individual had to first of all be quick: quick in reacting to the attack of a predator and in gaining an escape route, in deciding how to pursue prey, in making use of territory that others were utilizing at that same moment, in the selection of a partner and of a place in which to take refuge, and so forth. But speed on its own would have been insufficient. Decisions of such importance also had to be, if not perfect, at least of sufficient quality to guarantee acceptable results, even though competition with other individuals would inevitably have influenced the level of satisfaction to which a human being could aspire and also the speed with which a solution could be achieved.

In order to better understand the primitive decision making process, one can imagine an individual looking for food in a territory populated by other individuals. If the number of individuals similar to him/herself was not excessive, he/she could look for food, distinguish the edible food from that which was inedible, and have enough time to eat his/her fill. If, however, that territory was overpopulated, then the old strategies of choice would be completely ineffective, because others would be exhausting the available food supply. The only solution would be to make the quickest decision possible, to be faster than the competitors and to make the best use of the available information. Naturally this second solution would entail advantages but also risks, such as making provisions of inedible food. In any case, the quick decision, even if made on the basis of scarce but fundamentally correct information, would prove to be the winning one.

For the purposes of survival these factors — correctness of interpretation and speed of decision — are decisive. But in fact the general economy of the mind avails itself of both slowness and rapidity in carrying out the operations essential to survival, such as measuring quantities and distances. Without the use of efficient and effective cognitive strategies which allow for the choosing and the simplifying of problems within brief time limits, our processing of information would not have been (and would not be) successful. Such strategies that reduce the time needed to make decisions have been essential tools for the successful functioning of the cognitive economy of our species. These strategies have, in fact, enabled us to face the limits of our mind (minimizing the effort necessary to make decisions) and to respond to the most pressing internal and external necessities (accumulating rapidly, directly or by inference, the information necessary to make decisions).

Therefore, if it is true that evolutionary pressure urged the human mind to accumulate information to provide the basis for making rational decisions, the vast majority of human choices have been made using quick and simple decision strategies. It is probable that these strategies developed as a result of human cognitive limitations (and from their influence on human knowledge of reality), from human drive, and from environmental pressures. The adaptive value of these strategies was revealed in the use of the natural resources supplied by the environment, the strategies proving to be not only remarkably flexible when humans faced new situations, but also ecological, as they tended to result in the suitable use of environmental resources.

The strategies just described have little to do with the procedures of rationality in the tradition that goes from Aristotle to Frege. But in fact these strategies are used by systems with a high adaptive value and provide results which are generally better that those generated by sophisticated algorithms which are more costly from a computational point of view. Naturally, elegant as it may be, this *evolutionary model of rationality* does not clarify how animals (and, with notable distinction, also human beings) can easily face new situations. These adaptive capacities must now confront a significant difficulty in the management of new situations, a difficulty completely attributable to the specificity of our cultural and genetic evolution, which has not prepared us to face critical aspects of the environment which derive from the high degree of human control of the planet.

It must be said that our ancestors gradually passed from *horizontal* cultural transmission, i.e. imitation of similar individuals, which is characteristic of other species, to *vertical* cultural transmission, i.e. transmission from one generation to another. Vertical cultural transmissions has obvious advantages, but does require a substantial continuity between one generation and the next. In fact, if there is a discontinuity between generations it can come to pass that the younger generation receives knowledge and strategies which are inadequate for the new environment. Certainly the flexibility and the adaptability of our mind, together with some degree of horizontal cultural transmission, can rectify such a discontinuity. But what happens when there is a sudden reversion to principally horizontal cultural transmission? It is reasonable to presume that responses would be strongly influenced by mimetic behaviours of the majority or of successful individuals.

In a large number of decision-making processes the brain does not use general models — which would be difficult and time-consuming, and not always adaptable to specific decision-making problems — but rather a sort of *natural logic* of inferential strategies, conscious or subconscious. This system is quite different, as said before, from *formal logic*, and its "rules", though certainly fallible and less rigorous, have shown themselves, since the beginning of the species, to be adaptively more effective. Thanks to theoretical studies and to experimental research into the *psychology of decision making*, the idea that formal tables of inference exist in the mind which are able to lead to valid conclusions regardless of the premises has been proven false. It has in fact been observed that individuals do not rely on innate formal rules of inference, but rather on their ability to understand the premises of a line of reasoning.

These conclusions have had very important consequences: on the one hand they have revealed the fallacy of the theory of a perfect rationality, while on the other they have highlighted the role played by factors such as unpredictability and uncertainty in individual economic decisions. Herbert Simon was among the first to confute the theory of *normative rationality* — according to which the rational decision maker maximizes the *expected benefit* — pointing out how, in conditions of uncertainty, such rationality is not evident in the actual behaviour of individuals. As a matter of fact, every time unexpected variables intervene between an ideal decision maker and the environment, such a model reveals itself to be inadequate.

The *anti-normative* character of Simon's theory expresses itself in the concept of *bounded rationality*, according to which the decision maker, because of his/her cognitive limits, adopts simplified models in the solution of problems. It is important to consider, moreover, that distorted representations and perceptions of risk strongly influence the decision-making process. Variables of this type — generated by chaotic and fluctuating conditions — make optimal responses highly improbable. In addition to the objective data at hand — statistical information on adversity, competitors, accidents and so on — subjective and inter-individual factors also impinge on the decision-making timelines; these factors include the willingness to assess and undertake risks, the impact of the environment, the fear of possible future consequences, the courage of the decision maker, and so on. Further, numerous analyses of risk perception have shown that human risk assessment is subjective and complex, very distant from rational calculations. In the majority of cases, in evaluating the risk the decision maker does not have sufficient statistical data or other information available. In some cases, then, the individual calls upon information and knowledge deriving from his/her experience, from casual news, from specialized knowledge, or from prejudices and suppositions. In other cases, the individual relies on deductions based on what he/she perceives at the moment, on the urgency of the situation, on what the individual remembers, or has heard, or has already attempted in situations involving the same sources of risk.

The great differences between models of rational decision making and the concrete behaviour of individuals can be explained by the presence of distorted rules of inference and decision-making criteria, determined by the interference of cognitive elements and of context in the evaluation of the problem and of the available information. It is the undeniable merit of Kahneman and Tversky to have recognized the causes of suboptimal decisions, both in the ploys and in the contrivances of thought with which the individual processes information, as well as in the representation of the problem. Their research shows how individuals tend to interpret events not through reasonable, objective, and verified assessments, but according to the experiences they first recall, more structured memories, or fear.

It has been noted that the reasoning of ordinary individuals in conditions of uncertainty is similar to reasoning founded on supposed certainties. In reality, when the mind constructs one or more models that define the context or the problem, each possibility represents an equal alternative. Immersed in the formulation of their own mental models, decision makers do not concentrate on the implicit information, but rather on the explicit information of such models. This could explain some of the oversights and distractions that cause accidents which are sometimes serious or deadly. It must also be said, then, that in the decision-making process efforts to *bring the problem into focus* themselves generate considerable distortions. Individuals, in fact, tend to create alternative models of action or inaction. In order to reach a decision, one focuses one's attention on the possible outcomes of that particular action, looking for evidence that validates a certain course of action, but avoiding the search for detailed information on the different alternatives. Even in everyday life, in situations in which one must make decisions without significant risks (such as buying one product or another, going to see a certain film or not), and when one is faced with a predominant option and an absence of significant alternatives, there emerges a spontaneous tendency towards *focalization* on that predominant option: a tendency which contrasts with the ideal of the decision maker, before deciding, rationally examining the alternatives. An appreciation of the tendency to *focalization* is important in understanding that the human mind operates in a way very different from rigid, rationalist formalisms. A person who ignores the alternatives is unable to consider and compare the advantages and disadvantages of the different choices.

There is an additional element to consider. Various studies have shown that excessive trust in one's own judgements arises from the tendency to look for proof in favour of an initial idea rather than evidence to the contrary. When people are instead forced, before expressing their own judgement, to consider the pros and cons of the decision to be made, this propensity is reduced. Often excessive trust in one's own judgements betrays the decision maker's ignorance of information available at the moment of decision making, and of other information necessary to the making of decisions relating to uncertain and risky situations. Another source of problems is statistical data, which are generally considered to be objective and a good basis for making economic and other decisions, but which all too often reveal themselves to be fallacious and illusory. Many problems derive from believing statistical data to be a kind of *objective photograph of reality* which reflects the "plain facts" and excludes any subjective evaluation. In fact, the chosen criteria and perceived probabilities are almost always different from a reality which is many-sided and dynamic, and which cannot be represented well by mathematical systems. As Darrell Huff demonstrated in his classic book *How to lie with statistics*, not only do statistical data not photograph reality, they often deform it. In this sense, common statistical procedures, rather than providing a tool for living with uncertainties, tend to create new "illusions of certainty" or even "false certainties". In contrast to what is widely believed, numbers hardly ever "speak for themselves"; rather, they almost always support the position of the person presenting the numbers. "Reading" and "interpreting" the data of reality is essential to decision making in many fields of human activity. In medicine, for example, diagnoses and care are very often delivered on the basis of statistical data; and in the legal domain DNA tests and some statistical data are accepted as proof of guilt during trials. In difficult cases such as situations of uncertainty, our behaviour — as Gerd Gigerenzer has pointed out — distances itself systematically from the predictions of normative models of decision making. What is more: such behaviour shows an irrational characteristic that — in the presence of information which has not been analyzed critically — can make a bad situation worse, with potentially dramatic consequences, in particular for the work of doctors and lawyers.

According to Gigerenzer the calculation of probability makes both the overcoming of the illusion of certainty and the rational acceptance of uncertainty possible. Guiding us in our uncertainty is a *logic of the uncertain* made up of rules of action and of rational assessment based on the laws of probability. This logic is held to be at the foundation of a *probabilistic conception of the mind*, of which an essential part is what is known as *Bayesian reasoning*, in which the probability of a cause must be deduced from an observed effect. This reasoning prompts us to re-examine our beliefs and specifically our attributions of probability. In this way, according to Gigerenzer, we could soon reach a *second probabilistic revolution* which would convert the image of an omniscient mind into a more plausible one of a *limited mind* able to generate effective decisions in conditions of uncertainty. In this model we could achieve a more accurate understanding of the data with which we are presented, our environment, and also the limits of our rationality.

Despite its undeniable appeal, such a hypothesis presents considerable problems. The primacy assigned by Gigerenzer to *uncertainty* excludes the theoretical relevance of probability from an account of rational behaviour, and by the same token, the very idea of a *logic of uncertainty*. He is convinced that the incapability to reason in probabilistic terms results from representations of risk which are difficult to interpret. In other words, individuals commit fewer errors in the evaluation of data when the information is presented to them in familiar and concrete terms, rather than in conditional terms or in terms of probability. It follows that if before learning to reason in a different way was believed to be useful in order to correct specific "irrationalities", now by relying on *quick and frugal heuristics* it is possible to reformulate the data according to a different model.

Gigerenzer has described all of the strategies with which each organism is equipped as an *adaptive toolbox*: a toolbox whose instruments are precisely those various heuristics. In other words, the toolbox is a repertory of heuristics with which each species is equipped at a particular moment of its evolution. Each one of us chooses to use the heuristic best suited to the specific task at hand, just as a blacksmith chooses from among his tools the one that is most suitable for the work in which he is engaged. In some cases one initially choses the wrong heuristic or tool, but this can be changed during the execution of a task. The "toolbox" has a set of simple heuristics, designed for quick and easy application; indifferent to formal coherence, but oriented rather towards adaptive effectiveness; well suited to the environment in which they evolved; and helpful in the solution of problems linked to the challenges presented by the environment (procuring food, avoiding predators, finding a partner and a safe refuge, but also, on a higher level, exchanging goods, realizing profits, and so on). Such tools work well in natural situations, where the constraints in terms of time, knowledge and computational capacities make the adoption of quick and efficient strategies a preferable and winning solution. The toolbox is regulated by motivations and emotional impulses. In addition, it must be equipped with learning models for the application of heuristics to unusual and unforeseen situations that derive from changes in the environment.

In order to describe the nature of the "toolbox", Gigerenzer adopted the metaphor of a mechanic and salesman of used car parts in a remote region, who, not possessing all of the tools or parts he needs to fix a vehicle, invents solutions with what he has available. In order to solve the problem the mechanic will first try one thing and if that does not work he/she will try another and then another, until, using everything at his/her disposal, an appropriate solution is found to the problems that present themselves on each occasion. In the "toolbox" there are also the means for constructing new heuristics which can then be reutilized when a similar situation arises. Gigerenzer considers three main types of rules which govern the decision-making process: *searching rules*, which direct the search for alternatives (the set from which to choose) and for the cues (the considerations on the basis of which the alternatives are evaluated); *rules of termination*, which establish when to terminate the search for alternatives and cues; and *rules of decision making*, which direct the choice between the alternatives. But we will expand upon this further ahead.

# 2

# At the Origin of the Concept of Decision Making

## Historic passages

How does our mind behave in choosing between various alternatives? Few other questions have occupied to the same degree the attention of philosophers, psychologists and economists of every age. The first attempts to analyse decision making appear in ancient Greek thought, in most cases as a part of discussions of the logical procedures which allow the individual to make inferences and to draw conclusions from specific premises, on the basis of which both individuals and groups reason, establish scientific theories and determine courses of action. In *Nicomachean Ethics*, Aristotle defines the decision-making process as a *deliberate appetition*, which is a logical and psychological sequence that starts with desire, continues with volition and concludes with the act of choice.

Many centuries later, first medieval philosophers (primarily Scholastic philosophers who refashioned the categories of Aristotelian logic) and then Humanist and Renaissance philosophers took a renewed interest in the ways individuals choose and on the exercising of human beings' free choice. During the seventeenth century the growing faith in rationality favoured the progress of empirical research — as is well known, the theories of Copernicus, Galileo, Kepler and Newton promoted the birth of the hypothetical-deductive method and, therefore, of modern science — and also encouraged some philosophers and scientists, one century later, to believe that eventually science would reveal every secret of nature. The principal inspirer of this belief was René Descartes, according to whom philosophy must use a method of deduction similar to that used in mathematics. He maintained that only a system of knowledge based on fundamental certitudes, such as the rational certainty of one's own existence, can give human beings shelter from the tricks of unanalysed information derived from perception. Human beings can doubt everything except for their own existence, which existence is demonstrated by the act of thinking.

Those long chains composed of very simple and easy reasonings, which geometers customarily use to arrive at their most difficult demonstrations, had given me occasion to suppose that all the things which can fall under human knowledge are interconnected in the same way. And I thought that, provided we refrain from accepting anything as true which is not, and always keep to the order required for deducing one thing from another, there can be nothing too remote to be reached in the end or too well hidden to be discovered. [Descartes, 1985, p. 120]

Descartes was convinced that, if we could eliminate each and every element of emotional interference, the logical-deductive process would lead knowledge and that philosophy to peaks that until then had been the exclusive privilege of the *sciences of nature* [Mirowski, 1989]. This is the origin of that dualistic philosophy, according to which knowledge arises exclusively from the mind (and not through the union of mind and body), and which for a long time has influenced our concept of knowledge and our ways of knowing. In other words, we do not perceive external objects through our senses — that is, by the sequence of nerve impulses that pass from receptors to nerves to thalamus and finally to the brain — but exclusively through the pathway of the intellect. It is not by chance that Descartes considered perception to be an obscure function, something that originated in the confused mingling of mind and body, and held that "knowledge" deriving from the senses such as sight, touch, hearing was often flawed.

Against the thesis that the only criteria of truth and knowledge are the clear and distinct ideas of our intellect, stands the philosophy of Blaise Pascal in France. According to Pascal, pure rationality is not achievable in this world, which by nature is filled with uncertainties, doubts and contradictions. Pascal bitterly criticizes Descartes' attempt to demonstrate the existence of God through the *method of doubt*, and also derides his concept of God as "motor of the universe", calling this the "God of philosophers".

In the cultural atmosphere that followed the Reformation and the Counter-Reformation it was Pascal who caused a new and more measured conception of the power of reason to emerge, a conception that recognized uncertainty as an extremely important and inescapable component of human life. This contributed significantly to shaking the belief that ordinary human reasoning could be brought to the same level as formal logical inferences. Around 1654, in a famous letter to the mathematician Fermat on problems of gambling, Pascal puts forward the thesis that at the foundation of rationality is the notion of probability. This is the first and a very illuminating attempt to consider the presence of uncertainty in an analysis of decision making, and to that recognize decision must be addressed with new methods that recognize that it proceeds according to different rules than formal logic. With regard to the question of God's existence, Pascal imagines that each individual finds him/herself faced with a sort of bet: to decide whether God exists or not, and asks:

> What will you wager? According to reason, you can do neither the one thing nor the other; according to reason, you can defend neither of the propositions. [Pascal, 1910, p. 84]

Choosing, then, is never an arbitrary act. Each one of us must decide to live as though God existed or as though he did not exist. We have only two possibilities. Not deciding, or not wanting to believe, also constitutes a choice. Now, it is clear that we do not have any certainty regarding the existence of God. Our decision is not and cannot be based on certain premises known beforehand, from which to deduce through reasoning a conclusion which would also be certain, but rather on probabilistic premises, on a search for the value and utility of different possibilities. This concerns, in other words, the carrying out of a calculation in order to evaluate which of the two options is more useful and convenient for the beatitude of humankind, evaluating advantages and disadvantages, and considering the overall value of each option. In the end, according to Pascal, the difference in the values of the two options is so great as to make the decision predictable: on one plate of the scale there is something infinite (eternal salvation), and on the other, something finite (life on earth). In the calculation of utility infinite quantities outweigh finite ones. The problem is analogous to that presented by a new scientific discovery which opens the path to a technological innovation, namely, the decision of whether or not to use, make known, or manufacture the technological innovation. Not introducing an innovation that could benefit many people is a choice which no doubt has disadvantages as well as advantages. A real decision of this type has more than two options — and thus is then more complicated than Pascal's decision about God — because it involves a range of alternatives between two extremes. Another difference is that the values in play are not infinite, and therefore the decision is less predictable than in the case proposed by Pascal. Nonetheless the problem has sufficient analogies to allow us to consider Pascal as the starting point for a new type of probabilistic reasoning which concerns the making of decisions in conditions of risk.

In the same period in England, while Thomas Hobbes [2008] maintains that individual choice derives from the calculation of what is useful and what is harmful, John Locke [1690] resolutely denies the universality and infallibility of reason. According to Locke, not even the most rational individual makes a decision in the pure light of certainty, but rather among the shadows of uncertainty. With a charming image, the English philosopher likens reason as a candle that illuminates our path, but gives off a dim light incapable of illuminating everything. According to Spinoza [2008], on the other hand, decision making is an attribute of thought, deducible from the laws of motion and immobility, in which free will concedes its place to a continuous conative activity which analyses objects and determines their desirability automatically.

In the work of later philosophers rationality assumes the role of an instrument of critique, of a "lamp" that illuminates every philosophical, moral or religious category, highlighting their incongruities. With a radical critical revision of metaphysical rationalism, David Hume reaches a scepticism that does not spare important psychological and moral problems. In his *Dialogues on natural religion* [1779], he affirms that there is no reason why the "little agitation of the brain" that we call thought should be elevated to a universal model. He also emphasizes that a healthy philosophy should protect itself from any such illusion. Reason is always subordinate to passions [Hume, 1739] and it will never be possible to separate reason from them. The thoughts of this Scottish philosopher exercised great influence on the research that followed. Kant, in particular, gave him credit for having interrupted a long "dogmatic slumber" of philosophy and for having succeeded in harmonizing the principles of empiricism with rationalistic issues, paving the way for further developments in critical philosophy.

In his *Critique of pure reason* [1781] Kant maintains the necessity of an "ideal" court in which reason can play, at the same time, the role of supreme judge granted it by the Enlightenment as well as the role of the accused. The task of reason is to define the areas of human knowledge and to police attempts to violate the limits of these areas. But in order to do this, reason is paradoxically forced to put itself "on trial". This is where the Kantian critique finds its roots: it is a critique of any form of dogmatism or metaphysical knowledge, and, at the same time, a search for the limits and the possibilities of human rationality. If for Kant decision making must conform to the law, for rationalists of the second half of the 1900s it became an act which encompasses in itself reason, sentiments and emotions.

## Moral arithmetic and the marginalist revolution

Around the middle of the eighteenth century, research on human rationality went beyond the exclusive domain of philosophy in order to address the subject from a broader perspective. Accepting the *principle of utility* as a general criterion of human action, philosophers of the Utilitarianist and Individualist schools provide new interpretive keys for human behaviour and, therefore, for economic conduct. In looking at behaviour, Utilitarianist philosophers consider the result and the practical effect of actions, without, as in Kantian ethics, dwelling on the formal analysis of the intentions of human action. It is no coincidence that Jeremy Bentham [1988], the founder of the Utilitarianism, defined *moral arithmetic* as the calculation on the basis of which everything that increases one's well-being corresponds to utility. A theoretical premise of utilitarianism is that the search for individual gain involves, on a wider scale, in increase in social well-being (the Smithian *invisible hand*), and that this effect renders plausible the idea that individual gain has moral value. According to Bentham, society is an aggregate of individual interests governed by an *instrumental rationality* which is set on defining the most suitable and efficient means for reaching specific ends.

It is the *neoclassical* or *marginalist* theory, usually traced back to the pioneering writings of Daniel Bernoulli, which introduces the psychological concept of "subjective value". This concept introduces the distinction between the *expected value* of a result (objective value) and its *expected utility* (subjective value). In a famous essay in the journal *Econometrica* [Bernoulli 1954/1738], the Swiss mathematician emphasises that it is not enough to calculate the "expected value" by multiplying the estimated value of each event by the probability that it will occur, then dividing the sum of these products by the total number of possible cases. In fact, the value of an object depends not on the benefits it produces, but only on the utility that it procures.

> The price of the item is dependent only on the thing itself and is equal for everyone; the utility, however, is dependent on the particular circumstances of the person making the estimate. Thus there is no doubt that a gain of one thousand ducats is more significant to a pauper than to a rich man though both gain the same amount. [Bernoulli, 1954/1738, p. 24]

Through the concept of *decreasing marginal utility*, which Bernoulli used to solve the famous "Paradox of St. Petersburg" [Shapley, 1977, Samuelson, 1977], the scale of preferences transforms itself into a continuous function in which the marginal utility increases with the possession of a good and decreases with the quantity possessed. In this sense, the *maximization* of *the expected utility* of wealth, or the "moral expectation", constitutes a sensible rule of decision making for choices that involve significant risk. The creation of the concept of *marginal utility* constituted a decisive moment for the "marginalist revolution" and for the birth of the neoclassical theoretical system centred on the notions of *utility* and *self-interest*, which was first fully elaborated in the research of Jevons [1871], Menger [1871] and Walras [1874]. At about the same time, but in different places and with different methods, Jevons (through empirical work), Menger (through logical-deductive reasoning) and Walras (through mathematics) tried to respond to the general dissatisfaction with the *classical value-work theory* (as stated by Adam

Smith, David Ricardo, John Stuart Mill and Karl Marx), and reconsidered the role of the utility of goods in the determination of their value.

In the second half of the nineteenth century and the first half of the twentieth, marginalist theory drove scholars such as Maffeo Pantaleoni, Friedrich von Hayek, Heinrich Gossen, Maurice Allais and others to investigate into the relationship between psychology and economics, leaving behind, in a manner of speaking, the classical paradigm founded on value-work. The analysis of subjective factors, based on the importance attributed by the agent to a certain product, enriched the links between psychology and economics, even if the dominance of economics (an epistemologically "strong" discipline by virtue of its sophisticated mathematical language) continued to prevail. The declaration of Ludwig von Mises, according to whom economics begins where psychology ends [von Mises, 1959], restored of the general faith in economics as a rigorous science, and as a science that is explicative, predictive and altogether separate from psychology. Lionel Robbins, in *An Essay on the Nature and Significance of Economic Science*, famously defined economics as a "science which studies human behaviour as a relationship between ends and scarce means which have alternative uses" [1935, pp. 16–17], and thus effectively stilled all doubts regarding the "scientific" nature of economic research. The use of an axiomatic approach of a mathematical type sets a solid basis for a markedly *normative* vision of rationality.

## Inflections of rationality

Since Aristotle, formal logic — that is to say, the study of rules that allow for the making of inferences and, therefore, the drawing of correct conclusions from premises — has been considered to be at the basis of both reasoning in everyday life (when we draw a conclusion from data, solve problems, make decisions, assess the coherency of our knowledge, and so on), and of the sciences and mathematics, where it is taken for granted that a correct argumentation must invariably follow the formal rules of logic [Legrenzi and Mazzocco, 1975].

The term *rationality* has assumed different meanings over the course of time: reason itself, reasonableness, the study of the form and procedures of reason, and coherence between a system of values and adopted objectives [Braine, 1978]. For theorists of decision making, rationality pertains to the choice of the most suitable means and conduct in order to pursue the goals that one proposes to reach. The criteria of rationality are, in fact, *coherence between thought and action* and *between means and end*; *transitivity* which allows one to pass from a plan to its execution by choices evaluated according to the order of their functionality (in such a way that if A is more functional than B, and B than C, then A is preferred to C), and *optimization*, which allows one to reach a goal with the least possible expenditure of time, effort, or money. This, naturally, requires both the most ample information possible on the alternatives, and a certain amount of creativity, especially when there is a significant imbalance between the availability of information and of processing power and the complexity of the situation in which one finds oneself [Bencivenga, 1985].

*Reasoning* can be defined as the procedure (or the sum of procedures) through which reason operates: procedures of inference, argument, conclusion, induction, deduction, analogy and still more. In other words, it is the sum of mental processes by which inferences are drawn and new knowledge is expanded starting from a set of premises or given knowledge [Girotto, 1994]. Classically, reasoning has been subdivided into two categories: *deductive*, when one passes from the general to the particular; and *inductive*, when one passes from the particular to the general. One can say that in deductive inferences the conclusions are already implicitly present in the premises: new informational knowledge is not generated, and something that is already implicitly known is expressed in a different way. On the contrary, in inductive inferences the conclusions are not present in the premises, and the conclusion reveals something about reality that was not known previously. It is obvious that with inductive inferences, in contrast with deductive inferences, one cannot draw conclusions that are valid from the point of view of logic [Lemmon, 2008]. A further element of classification concerns the nature of the premises. Before making an inference, already existing knowledge can be certain or probabilistic. In other words, the premises can be affirmations that are certain in an absolute way or that are probably true with a greater or lesser margin of certainty. Reasoning from premises of this second type is referred to as *probabilistic reasoning*. A probabilistic inference can be either deductive or inductive. Therefore, three categories of *non-probabilistic deductive reasoning* can be identified. For the purposes of our investigation the reasoning mechanisms at the basis of decision making are important, as this is an activity in which probabilistic as well as deductive inferences are made [Girotto, 1994]. Of the different theories of reasoning here we will consider the *theory of mental logic*, the *theory of mental models* and the *heuristics and biases program*.

**(1)** The *theory of mental logic* assumes that formal tables of inference exist in the mind, which, regardless of the content of the premises, lead to valid conclusions. This is the ancient Aristotelian idea according to which logic and thought coincide, which was undisputed until around the middle of the nineteenth century, when the rules of formal logic were still the normative terms of reference for assessing the human mind. Even after the work of Frege brought an end to this theory, researchers in psychology continued to identify logic (or at least a part of logic) with reasoning for another century. Since the 1970s modified versions of the theory have been proposed, versions that specify that the rules of inference are applied to the premises as these are interpreted by the subjects, on the basis both semantic and practical considerations.

(2) The *theory of mental models*, developed at the end of the twentieth century from the pioneering works of P. Johnson-Laird [1983], begins with a notion of mental representation founded on models, and with the assumption that the human mind is not already equipped with formal rules of inference, but that individuals put their trust in their ability to understand the premises of a line of reasoning [Legrenzi and Girotto, 1996]. On the basis of this understanding and of general knowledge people construct mental models of the states of things described in any natural language. According to Johnson-Laird, errors are explained by the constraints imposed by the limits of memory. This theory, initially developed for deductive reasoning, has subsequently also been applied to inductive and decisional reasoning [Girotto, 2004, pp. 103–28].

The theory of mental models allows us to shed light on the illusions of reasoning [Legrenzi, Girotto and Johnson-Laird, 2003]. The discovery that people make incorrect inferences is a significant problem for the theory of mental logic. In fact, if one follows the rules of logic one can only make valid inferences: one reaches true conclusions if the premises are true, and false conclusions if the premises are false (regardless of the contents of the premises). According to the theory of mental models, we do not think beginning with objects or events present in the external world or in our mind, but with descriptions of those objects or events in the form of mental representations [Tversky, 2004]. The latter are influenced both by the description of the objects or events, and by constraints in the functioning of the human mind. Many "absences of reasoning" can be explained in this way, namely those slip-ups and mistakes which have contributed to accidents large and small throughout history [Legrenzi, Girotto, Johnson-Laird, 1993].

In light of these considerations we must ask: in which conditions can the principles of scientific rationality be considered useful approximations of human reasoning? Moreover: if people agree on the plausibility of the theory of rational choice, why do they at times systematically move away from it, that is, why do they make irrational choices? Starting in the second half of the twentieth century it became clearer and clearer that rationality could not support itself on cognitive structures of enormous calculatory strength. Scholars tried, therefore, to develop a more realistic theory of rational behaviour, diluting the classical criteria of optimization. It was observed, in particular, that people do not try to pursue optimal solutions, but they settle instead for "satisfactory" strategies, in a sort of compromise between ideal reasoning and the inherent limits of the human mind (limits of perception, attention, calculation, memory, and reasoning) [Byrne, 2005, Byrne and Tasso, 1999]. Other constraints on the application of the principles of rationality include the imperfection of the circumstances in which choices are made and reasoning is carried out. All of the necessary information for optimal decision-making is almost never available; indeed, we often find ourselves facing situations in which information is uncertain and/or incomplete [Legrenzi, Girotto, Johnson-Laird, Sonino, 2003].

Let us consider our way of reasoning when we have to choose a bottle of wine. How do we go about "rationally" choosing the best wine in relation to our needs and means? If the objective were to choose the best bottle of wine, then we would have to try every available wine in order to find the best one. Naturally such a procedure is impractical. In cases of this type, faced with uncertainty, we trust the rules learned from popular knowledge: the classification of wine on the basis of the label, the colour, the vintage, the price, and the consumption advice. We apply, that is to say, rules based on general principles which obviously do not give us the certainty of success, but very often work. In reasoning and in decisions we apply heuristic procedures — probably fallible because they are only approximations of "perfect rationality" — but certainly practical [Tversky 2004].

(3) The *heuristics and biases program*, introduced in 1982 by Kahneman, Slovic and Tversky, is used for the analysis of probabilistic and decisional reasoning. According to this theory the inferences of inexpert subjects depend upon the activation of non-systematic problem-solving procedures — heuristics — the use of which does not always guarantee the reaching of a normatively correct solution, but which, on the contrary, provokes systematic errors (*biases*) in some cases.

While the first two theories are traditionally applied to deductive reasoning, the third deals with the issues of judgement and of decision making. The *heuristics and biases program*, initially conceived to explain the processes of judgement and decision making in conditions of uncertainty, was subsequently applied to probabilistic reasoning [Tversky, 2004]. Now, it is clear that any general theory which deals with reasoning is not immune to theoretical problems. In the case in question, there are essentially three important problems. First, there is the *problem of competency*. In the past it was believed that people, even when they lacked specific knowledge of formal logic, were able to adhere to this logic in their reasoning; recently it has been discovered that our inferences, both in everyday situations and in experimental ones, are exposed to numerous systematic errors and we therefore move away from the inferences predicted by the normative principles of logic or by statistics [Johnson-Laird, 1983; Johnson-Laird, Legrenzi and Girotto, 2004]. Secondly, there is the *explanation of these errors*. Thirdly, there is the *effect on reasoning of the contents of the premises and of the context in which these are presented*. In fact, the performances of subjects differ in the face of problems that have the same formal structure but are presented in different versions [Legrenzi, Girotto, Johnson-Laird, 1993, Legrenzi, 1998].

## On limited rationality

It is probable that animals, occupied in every instant of their lives with challenges posed by the environment, do not ask themselves whether their choices are right or wrong. They just take action. It is the task of nature to "promote" their actions according to their adaptive success. In other words, the choices are "right" if the organism survives, develops and reproduces with success. Animals, however, live in a world that requires rapid choices, in which a somewhat inferior decision made rapidly is better, that is, offers higher survival value, than a hypothetically superior decision made more slowly. In a different way, our behaviour is the result of the critical and self-critical functions of the mind (an "organ" with computational capacities and a finite memory) that evolution has made available to us. In addition to possible errors in reasoning, the mind is able to retain only a limited amount of information in its long-term memory, and even less in its short-term memory. Moreover, its capacity to process this information requires time and is effective only up to a certain level of complexity. The external environment also imposes severe restrictions, especially of a temporal nature: decisions must be made before those of potential competitors. This implies a limitation in the search for cues from the environment that can help us solve our problems.

Let us consider the following decision scenarios:

- Decisions in the presence of known values for each alternative which do not involve probabilities (for example, for the purchase of a house, in which for each of the alternatives one knows with exactitude the price, the distance from work or school, the dimensions, and so on);
- Decisions in the presence of probability or conditions of risk, typical of most situations of everyday life; and
- Decisions in conditions of certainty and decisions in conditions of risk — that is to say, when we are not even able to assign a probability to each one of the possible outcomes of a specific action. These decisions are particularly important and also common, because in life very few decisions are made in conditions of certainty. The majority of human decisions, in fact, involve a certain degree of uncertainty which varies

from risk to ignorance [Resnik, 2003]. Here it is possible to distinguish decisions in conditions of risk (when in the basic information the probabilities are also present) from decisions in conditions of uncertainty (when in the basic information the probabilities are not present). [Hempel, 1986; Harsanyi, 1986]

Not all authors make the same distinction between risk and uncertainty. For some, the concept of risk should be limited to particular types of attributions of probabilities [Knight, 1960]; for others, there is no difference between risk and uncertainty, or at most, the words reflect different types of uncertainty, measurable in probabilities which reflect the degrees of trust that the subject puts into different contexts. According to Lindley [1990] individuals always calculate probabilities, even when they find themselves facing situations in which calculations do not help to assign values to different outcomes or the differences are small.

There are other scholars who identify four categories — risk, uncertainty, ambiguity and ignorance — classifiable on the basis of the knowledge of the possible outcomes of each decision and of their probability of occurrence [Szekely, 1986]. It is possible to further distinguish:

(a) *decisions in conditions of certainty* (no need to consider probabilities);
(b) *decisions in conditions of risk* (known probabilities);
(c) *decisions in conditions of uncertainty* (probabilities unknown or difficult to determine).

These are the different types of decisions. In reality, the attribution of probability to an event is consistent with Lindley's conclusion that there is a *continuum* between situations of pure risk (known probabilities) and those that are more uncertain, in which the attribution of risk is more complex. In real situations — namely outside of gambling establishments and laboratories — the distinction between risk, uncertainty and ignorance is never clear-cut [Shackle, 1955]. Thus, making a decision in conditions of uncertainty means deciding which course of action to follow, among those that are possible, without any certainty of its possible consequences.

## Decisions in conditions of uncertainty and of risk

Theorists of decision making have for some decades been engaged in analysis of the logical-formal process of choosing in the presence of incomplete information and in conditions of risk or of uncertainty. The formal theory of decision making was introduced in the first half of the twentieth century by Abraham Wald [1950] and was developed above all for use with

Bayesian statistics [Savage, 1954] which had as their objective the definition of the best strategy on the basis of a predetermined criterion of optimality. Over the course of time, various types of optimal results were identified for the analysis of decision making strategies:

(a) the choice which minimizes the maximum loss (which calculates for each choice the maximum loss that could derive from it, opting for the minimum one);

(b) the choice which maximizes the maximum gain (which calculates for each choice the maximum gain that could derive from it);

(c) the choice which tends towards the smallest average loss (according to the criterion of Bayes–Laplace);

(d) the choice which tends towards the smallest average loss (according to the criterion of Bayes–Bernoulli).

A common characteristic of all of these strategies is that none of them uses probabilistic information. These strategies are used primarily in the theory of gambling, in order to define approaches that are careful or audacious by nature. If Dennis Lindley's idea is true, according to which an attribution of probability is nonetheless carried out, the strategies just described may appear to be not completely realistic compared to others which instead use probabilistic information. The total utility value of each choice is definable as the sum of the products of the value of each possible outcome of the alternative under examination and the probability that it will come to pass [Lindley, 1990]. In other words, each possible choice has a certain number of possible outcomes, each one of these has a certain probability of happening and to this we attribute a certain value (positive or negative). It is the task of the decision maker to maximize the expected value, that is, to choose the alternative associated with the highest expected value. In this sense, the choice that maximizes the expected value is rational and the models of reasoning and of decision making inspired by this choice are at the same time *normative* (because they specify what a person should do) and *descriptive* (because they explain how a person in fact reaches a certain decision).

Such a perspective was adopted by all those who saw a certain symmetry between human inferences and the laws of probability and of statistics; this view is still accepted by many researchers, albeit with significant variations, in the scientific domains of psychology, biology and economics. It must be said that, as opposed to artificial situations in which probabilities and values are usually known beforehand, the fact that roulette players (or players of other similar games) sometimes choose the alternative with the least expected value contrasts with the idea according to which they should adhere to the principle of maximization. In order to explain real-life decisions — which if judged on the basis of a purely objective theory of expected value would otherwise be incomprehensible — it was necessary to introduce two different hypotheses:

- when the calculation of probabilities does not provide precise cues, the probabilities are to be considered purely subjective;
- when the values of each outcome are uncertain, one substitutes them with a subjective estimate of utility.

In everyday life, a decision maker would have to analyze the situation in detail in order to maximize the expected utility, calculated by substituting the objective probabilities with the subjective ones, and the expected value with its corresponding expected utility. It is by considering this process that we can understand why people gamble, for example: it is in such a way that psychological aspects such as the pleasure and the thrill derived from gambling and the feelings derived from the denial of any monetary risk become integrated into the calculation of expected utility. According to this understanding of the decision process, each one of us would have to carry out, when faced with a real decision, a complex calculation which would include the collection of a large amount of information and of an enormous quantity of formulations for its processing. In brief, a decision maker would have to:

(a) list all of the possible actions, options and alternatives of action that he/she is faced with;
(b) know all of the possible outcomes of each action;
(c) consider all of the subjective probabilities of each consequence;
(d) determine every possible value (subjective utility) of each consequence;
(e) calculate without errors the expected utility of each action;
(f) carry out without errors the assessment of maximum utility.

Among the activities necessary for the maximization of expected utility one is particularly important: the calculation of the probabilities of each consequence. The other tasks, such as the complete search for all possible alternatives and consequences, potentially have an infinite dimension and are therefore much more complex to carry out. However, for a human decision maker the assessment of the probabilities of an event already constitutes quite an arduous task. In a famous *theorem* — introduced in an article entitled "Essay Towards Solving a Problem in the Doctrine of Chances" which was published posthumously in *Philosophical Transactions of the Royal Society of London* [1763] — Thomas Bayes laid down the mathematical basis both for the determination of probability subsequent to a given hypothesis on the basis of its prior probability, and for the gathering of eventual further information relevant to the objectives of that hypothesis. Bayes' theorem represents a normative reference for drawing the correct conclusions about the probabilities of an event subsequent to that given event. In reality, a large number of experiments have shown that individuals who are inexpert in statistics have a tendency not to modify probabilities beforehand, even when in the presence of pertinent information. When dealing with any error, people who are inexpert in statistics and in the calculation of probability encounter difficulty in determining probabilities subsequent to a given hypothesis. This consideration reveals more difficulties in the maximization of expected utility (especially if applied to inexpert individuals) in regards to the capacity to determine beforehand the outcomes of a certain action.

## The illusion of optimization

Let us now reconsider the layout of decision making in conditions of risk (or uncertainty) in relation to the classic economic model. Mention has been made of individuals' difficulty in assessing probabilities subsequent to a certain event, and of how this difficulty is only the least important of the difficulties that a real-life decision maker faces. The other problems which plague a decision maker include:

- identifying all of the possible courses of action;
- listing the possible consequences of each action;
- assigning a value to each possible outcome;
- assigning a probability to each possible outcome;
- correctly carrying out the calculation of the expected utility of each possible outcome; and
- determining the maximum utility which identifies the most convenient course of action.

Gary Klein [2001] analyzed these difficulties, which had been identified by experts of the field. The chief difficulties in working within the constraints required by a calculation are the non-exhaustive knowledge of the given conditions, the temporal limits, and finally the limits of memory and of calculation capabilities [Klein, 2001].

If there are several objectives in play it will not be only one single utility value that is associated with each consequence, but rather a sum of values for each possible objective. In addition, one will have to have at one's disposal both a rule for calculating the maximum utility (considering the different importance of the individual objectives), as well as a set of criteria for the evaluation of each objective. The situation becomes still more complex when one passes from a simple laboratory model into the real world: using formulas such as the *maximization of expected utility* in order to describe reasoning and decision making would be like adopting a simple mathematical formula in order to describe a complex physical system. This decision making system can work if the relevant variables are few (and the others insignificant), but it will be completely inadequate for complex, dynamic systems. Other methods are therefore necessary, methods which are drastically different from those used in the resolution of a system of algebraic-differential equations (expert systems, neural networks, computer simulation and others). Moreover, in a normal everyday decision the variables in play are often innumerable, or in fact infinite; there are very few cases in which a decision can be made on the basis of a limited number of measurable and verifiable factors.

As is by now evident, a significant number of difficulties confront the decision optimization model. Simon, moreover, has called attention to the necessity of being able to set a limit to the search for alternatives among which to choose: this search should come to an end once an alternative has been identified that satisfies the decision maker's aspiration level [Simon, 1990]. A similar "rule of conclusion" is necessary for the judgement criteria of the various alternatives. A second problem, emphasized by Klein [2001], is the difficulty in agreeing on an unambiguous definition of the term "optimization": in fact this term can refer to the optimization of the decision making process, as well as to the optimization of the decision itself. In turn, result optimization can refer to the best possible choice, or to the most advantageous choice given the information available. With regard to optimization of the method, the problem consists of understanding whether or not the best path for the desired solution has been followed, but in order to do this it would be necessary to have very precise points of reference and criteria for evaluation and comparison. More generally, "optimization" can simply refer to the best method for reaching an objective or may include additional factors to be considered in a given situation. From another point of view, optimization can take place at different levels: cognitive, behavioural, cultural or evolutionary [Pievani, 2005]. Naturally, the intersection of these four levels of optimization creates additional complexity in the making of individual choices, constrained as they are by the needs of the individual and those of the membership group. There is then the general *problem of infinite regression* tied to the necessity of introducing "rules of conclusion". Given the presence of so many constraints — the limits of memory, of the time in which to make a decision, of money, and of other types of resources to be used — it is necessary to establish a limit for the conclusion of a search. For example, one could assign a marginal value to the continuation of a search in order to compare it with further expected benefits. Or one could bring the search to an end when the costs for its continuation exceed the expected benefits. However, even this evaluation of the costs has its own cost and must, therefore, be added to the general calculation. But even this calculation has a cost to be added to the previous ones, and so on and so forth, in an infinite regression.

When one finds oneself faced with an unfamiliar problem, time for decision making is scarce and optimization is essentially impossible [Selten, 2001]. An individual who intends to maximize utility when facing a number of alternatives has limited decision-making time at his or her disposal. The individual, that is to say, must do his or her best in the time available. In this way, if the decision maker is familiar with the problem one presumes that he or she will be able to face it without having to devote considerable time or attention to it. When, instead, he or she has no familiarity with the situation, before making the final decision the decision maker must devise a method for identifying the alternatives among which to choose. Thus the individual is faced with a two-level decision making process: the first level consists in the identification of the alternatives among which to make a choice, and the second level consists in the choice of a method for facing the problems presented by the first level of decision making. Naturally, because of unfamiliarity, the problems presented by the first level also require energy. Therefore, a method is required for resolving the tasks imposed by the first level, and thus the decision making process acquires a third level. In such a way, one obtains an infinite sequence of levels. When time is limited, this infinite regression clearly makes it impossible to reach a decision using this procedure. In this sense, this process of optimization cannot optimize its own procedure.

According to Gödel's *incompleteness theorem* [1986; 1990], in every mathematical formalization powerful enough to axiomatize the elementary theory of natural numbers (that is to say, powerful enough to define the structure of natural numbers and govern the operations of sum and product), it is possible to construct a syntactically correct proposition which, from within that same system, can neither be demonstrated nor confuted. That is, a deductive system based on axioms cannot have the characteristics of coherence and completeness at the same time. If the derived theorems are not contradictory there is at least one indemonstrable theorem starting with those axioms, an undecidable case which one cannot determine to be true or false [Lolli, 2007]. If one chose to accept the undecidable theorem as an axiom, the problem simply gets moved and the new system will have another undecidable theorem. The difference between an axiom and a hypothesis can be seen in the fact that the non-admission of an axiom imposes an immediate halt to the analysis, while its admission produces consequences and theorems; on the contrary, accepting or not accepting a hypothesis can both be ripe with consequences [Berto, 2008]. Generally, a process of optimization, in which optimization also concerns the process itself, cannot be entirely optimized.

The concept just discussed is of great importance because, in the majority of cases, we find ourselves facing (and possibly resolving) unfamiliar problems in limited periods of time. In cases such as these, optimization is feasible only if the decision maker has the available data in front of him/her and therefore does not have to undertake a search for the necessary information. Gigerenzer [2001] has listed the following reasons why optimization can be achieved only in a limited number of situations, which do not generally present themselves in everyday life:

- if there are competing objectives, optimization can require very large computational resources;
- if there are incalculable objectives, reasons or cues, optimization can be impossible;
- if the alternatives are unknown and emerge only after a long search, optimization models, which function only for finite and known sets of choices, cannot be applied;
- if the cues or the reasons are unknown and require a long search process to discover, the optimization models, which are applied to finite and known sets of choices, are inapplicable;
- if the future consequences of the actions and of the events are unknown, the optimization models, which function for sets of finite and known consequences, are inapplicable;
- when an individual must make numerous decisions in real time, attempts at optimization can lead to paralysis by overwhelming the available computational resources.

Even if one were to enlist the aid of a computer in making decisions, the problem would still remain unsolved, because the computer would need information about all aspects of the decision, information that would therefore have to be known beforehand by the person who instructs the computer. Therefore, even if, thanks to their rapidity of calculation, the computer systems that support decisions can remedy some human limitations, the same problems that render optimization impossible still remain, problems such as infinite searching, regression, and ignorance of the relations between data. A computer simply does what we tell it to do at very high speeds; it cannot do what it has not been taught to do. There is an additional, intrinsic uncertainty: even supposing that one succeeds in providing perfect simulation models to the computer, the correctness of the resulting predictions depend on perfect knowledge of the initial conditions. This quite clearly reintroduces the problem of having accurate knowledge of all the data and of all the information, even if it might appear to be irrelevant: in short, the problem of an infinite search.

Optimization beforehand is, therefore, intrinsically impossible, unless one is endowed with infinite knowledge and infinite power of calculation, as is the case with *Laplace's demon*. Laplace was convinced that nature operated according to causal laws, which are reflected in the mathematical equations which describe it [Laplace, 1825]. This, however, does not imply the mechanical exactness of a prediction, but rather that an accurate prediction can be reached only by an *intellect* so vast that it knows with exactitude both the initial state of every single constitutive element of nature, and the forces acting on each one of these in a given instant, and also so vast that it can make calculations based on all of that data [Israel, 2004]. Naturally, the human mind is only a dim reflection of the *Laplacian intellect*: despite its desires and attempts to draw near to this type of intellect, the human mind will always remain infinitely far from it.

Laplace's philosophy has been the subject of a considerable number of misinterpretations that had the objective of demolishing the concept of determinism from the inside out. Scholars have attributed to him the suggestion that a perfectly deterministic prediction of events is possible, while in fact he says something quite different [Israel, 1996]. Laplace discusses this subject in the introduction to a treatise on probabilities, that is to say on a mathematical theory made necessary by our inability to attain a perfect understanding of the causal structure of phenomena [Ingrao and Israel, 1990]. On the other hand, the causality of phenomena is not the object of empirical verification, but an "obvious" metaphysical principle, traceable to the Leibnizian "principle of sufficient reason". It is exactly this essentially metaphysical nature of Laplacian causalism which makes it internally indestructible. It makes no sense, therefore, to search for internal contradictions to Laplace's argument. The many attempts to classify this argument as a sort of *strict predictive determinism*, with the implication that the ability to make perfect predictions would be attainable by humankind, are completely implausible [Israel, 1992].

Still more implausible are the attempts to demonstrate that even Laplace's intellect would be powerless when faced with the matter of prediction. It is said, for example, that although much more powerful than our own, Laplace's intellect could not determine with exactitude a number with infinite decimal digits, and that it would therefore fail when facing intrinsically uncertain elements in a measurement carried out in a finite period of time [Bertuglia and Vaio, 2003]. In truth, Laplace's intellect is not merely much more powerful than ours; it is immensely more powerful. Only this intellect is permitted — as only God or a demon is permitted — to identify with exactitude the initial state of a system and to follow the evolution thereof with perfect determination. The *uniqueness of solutions theorem* demonstrates that in a deterministic dynamic system, from a given initial state of only one subsequent state is possible at a given subsequent instant [Kline, 1980]. But the key point is that for certain systems that obey this theorem — such that for every point in space of the phases one and only one solution passes — the problem of prediction collides with the limits of human calculation (not to mention those of empirical analysis) which make the system chaotic. But the chaotic character of a system belongs to the epistemological level of the prediction, not to the ontological one. It is not by chance that one speaks of "deterministic chaos", in contrast with a determinism that would be contradicted by itself [Vulpiani, 1994]. The way in which Pierre Duhem phrased the question a century ago was very different because he spoke instead of mathematical deductions which are unusable by physicists. He states:

> ( . . . ) a mathematical deduction is of no use to the physicist so long as it is limited to asserting that a given rigorously true proposition has for its consequence the rigorous accuracy of some such other proposition. To be useful to the physicist, it must still be proved that the second proposition remains approximately exact when the first is only approximately true. And even that does not suffice. The range of these two approximations must be delimited; it is necessary to fix the limits of error which can be made in the result when the degree of precision of the methods of measuring the data is known; it is necessary to define the probable error that can be granted the data when we wish to know the result within a definite degree of approximation. [Duhem, 1954, p. 143]

Clearly, many factors exist which render the goal of optimization difficult to attain. On the other hand, if we were to renounce the goal of optimization how could we describe the decision making process in a way that was applicable to situations of everyday life? Would we have to give up on the idea of being rational individuals? And what value would our decisions have if there were no normative principle guiding them and guaranteeing their correctness? Ultimately, when we choose, how do we know that we have acted wisely?

## Heuristics and biases approach

In recent decades stress has often been placed on the fact that individuals inexpert in statistics make judgements and decisions not by applying the inferential rules of logic, but rather by applying less formal strategies that, on the one hand, can lead rapidly and efficiently to a result, but on the other hand can also prove misleading. These strategies can be thought of as types of algorithms, sequentially codified in our mind, which guide us to the solution of the problem, to a judgement or to a decision. Not only do these algorithms diverge significantly from formal logic, but they paradoxically depend on our very limits: limits that, when they lead to false conclusions, are considered flaws. In the 1970s Kahneman and Tversky, reviving an idea introduced by Herbert Simon in the mid-1950s, ascribed errors in reasoning to the application of heuristic strategies. The errors in question can for the most part be identified in laboratory situations, where individuals are faced with unnatural situations in which certain strategies can be successful and others (in different conditions) can fail. But what are the obstacles that one encounters in the resolution of problems? Here are a few:

- the order and the way in which information is presented;
- the nature of the task;
- the fact that the information is presented in probabilistic terms;
- the fact that the probabilities refer to single events (the Bayesian School) or to sequences of events.

In 1973 Kahneman and Tversky proposed the so-called lawyers and engineers problem, which became paradigmatic. Subjects were shown cards containing the description of a person and were told that the people described had been extracted from a sample of thirty engineers and seventy lawyers, even though the description suggested a profession different from the real one (for example, if the person was a lawyer, the description hinted that he or she was an engineer). Subsequently it was revealed to the subject that the card showed not a lawyer, but an engineer. In the experiment in question, the subjects identified the person on the card as an engineer more often than as a lawyer, therefore giving more credit to appearances than to the basic probabilities. It is interesting to observe that when the experiment was repeated without misleading descriptions, and the subjects had to identify the people on the cards exclusively on the basis of the probabilities, the subjects responded correctly. This experiment showed that the individuals tend to ignore the probabilities known beforehand in favour ot the evidence given afterwards (*base rate* neglect), confirming in this way the tendency to judge an individual as belonging to a certain category or class if he/she appears representative of such a category or presents characteristics typical of that class. In fact, guided by such a propensity, people tend to disregard other relevant information, such as basic probability [Tversky and Kahneman, 1974; Argyle, 1994].

With their *Heuristics and biases approach* Kahneman and Tversky pointed out that in the solution of problems, consumers adopt simplifications of a heuristic type completely different, at least on the surface, from *trade-off* training and utility maximization processes [Kahneman and Tversky, 1979; Schkade and Payne, 1994]. The experimental evidence suggest the existence of three main types of heuristic reasoning:

1. *The availability heuristic* leads us to predict the frequency or the probability of an event based on the facility with which an example comes to mind [Kahneman and Tversky, 1973], that is, to how "available" it is in the memory. "Hot" states of emotional excitement considerably increase the availability of thoughts tied to immediate emotions and to current needs, while they reduce the accessibility of other thoughts [Loewenstein, 1996]. One can understand, therefore, why such heuristics offer the advantage of a rapid simplification of assessments and prognoses that would otherwise be very complex. Nonetheless, such simplification can generate systemic errors. In fact, deciding on the basis of variables such as "familiarity", "emotive salience" and "temporal distance" can mean underestimating events that are less "sensational", but that are potentially more useful in providing us with important information for decision making. In fact there is no reason to believe that the most accessible characteristics are also the most relevant in the making of a good decision.

2. *The representativity heuristic* involves making decisions based on stereotypes [Shefrin and Thaler, 1992; Shefrin, 2000], and can be defined as the tendency of individuals to consider certain events as being representative of a class. In the making of judgements or assessments, individuals give too much importance to fact that an object or event belongs to a certain class and do not consider the real characteristics or probabilities of the situation. This excessive faith in stereotypes often leads to incorrect judgements.

3. *The anchoring and adjustment heuristic*: often in both economic choices and in everyday decisions, one directs one's calculations on the basis of a tacit initial reference defined as an *anchor* [Tversky and Kahneman, 1973]. It has been observed that individuals form their own assessments starting with an initial, arbitrary value, and later recalculate that value based on new information. Often, however, the adjustment is insufficient, and individuals dwell excessively on the initial value [Barberis and Thaler, 2003]. For example, if a person has to judge the capability, shyness or intelligence of another person, he/she will adopt as an *anchor* for the final judgement his/her own degree of capability, shyness and intelligence: consequently, the level of the person to be judged will be over- or underestimated.

In reality the heuristic "spectrum" is much wider and can also extend to other categories. For example, it can extend to *recognition heuristics*, which, when we are presented with two objects — one known and the other not — incline us to choose the familiar one (for example in deciding which of two cities is bigger, one chooses the city that one recognizes); to *imitation heuristics*, which lead us to choose what others do, the actions of the majority, or of those who have the greatest success; to *satisficing heuristics*, which make us accept the best level that can reasonably be aspired to in a given situation and which make us conclude a search as soon as a solution that satisfies that aspiration level is found; and to *means-ends analysis* which leads us to evaluate the difference between the present situation and the final situation that we wish to reach, gathering from memory things which, according to past experience, could be useful in reducing or cancelling out such differences. Other examples of these strategies are Kahneman's *elimination by aspects* and Tversky's *lexicographic heuristic*.

The *recognition heuristic* is one of a group of strategies defined as *non-compensatory*. These strategies operate such that one cue cannot be outweighed or compensated by a group of other less important cues. This heuristic represents the simplest case of *non-compensatory* strategy, because it leads to the making of a decision based on one cue without a search for other cues. One relies on what is, in fact, only a difference in the *recognition* of the alternatives available. The prototype of *non-compensatory* rules is represented by lexicographic strategies, in which in the analysis of the possibilities one follows some sort of orderly criterion. For example, in judging which is bigger between two numbers written in Arabic script with the same number of digits, one compares the digits one by one, starting with the first ones on the left and stopping as soon as one finds two numbers that are different.

Gigerenzer [2001] placed the *recognition heuristic* at the basis of other decision-making strategies. The experiment in which different people are asked which of two cities has the greatest population, giving them only small cues such as the presence of a professional soccer team in the highest league, is by now famous. The answer was guided by a strategy called the *take-the-best heuristic*, which is based on a very simple recognition heuristic. In brief, the people simply tried to recognize the name of a city, and looked no further. In this way, the answer was given on impulse and the recognized city was considered to be the biggest. If the first strategy failed, the people moved on to a second strategy. That is to say, they examined the cues one by one, and as soon as they found one in which the two cities showed a difference, they halted the reasoning process and declared that city to be the biggest which a single cue suggested might be larger [Czerlinski, Goldstein and Gigerenzer, 1999].

## The (im)possible solution

*The take-the–best heuristic* [Gigerenzer and Goldstein, 1996] is a brief algorithm with five stages, of which only the first involves the simple recognition heuristic:

1. Between two objects, one chooses the known one. If neither of the two is recognized, one chooses one at random. If both are recognized, one moves on to the second step;
2. The search for discriminating characteristics begins with the most salient characteristic of the two objects;
3. The rule of discrimination: the analyzed characteristic allows for the discrimination between the two objects;
4. If the characteristic allows for discrimination, then the operation ends and one chooses based on the value of the examined characteristic. Otherwise one returns to the second step and continues with the next characteristic;
5. If, in the end, it is impossible to discriminate based on the available information, the choice is made at random.

These heuristics, which show the impracticality of a decision-making *best way*, permit a more realistic description of the *modus operandi* of the individual decision-maker, shedding light on the importance of sensations, affections and emotions, dimensions long neglected because of their scarce "measurability". The incidence of such emotive aspects in the decision-making domain makes the urgency for a redefinition of the decision-making process clear. This process will have to be considered no longer as a calculation of utility, but rather a prediction made by a mind in a sensitive body [Berthoz, 2004]. In order to get as close as possible to a complete theory of human rationality it is necessary to understand what role emotion plays in it [Simon, 1988]. Emotions, attitudes and automatic affective evaluation represent the deciding factor of many judgements and behaviours [Kahneman and Ritov, 1994]. Slovic and his collaborators [2002] have pointed out how an affective reaction can constitute a heuristic factor in the evaluation of a wide variety of situations, even in the prediction of economic success in industrial sectors. In this sense, the so-called *affect heuristic* assumes particular importance, entering into play in the majority of sensorial-perceptive events and evoking "affective assessments" that are not always conscious.

> The failure to identify the affect heuristic much earlier, as well as its enthusiastic acceptance in recent years, reflect significant changes in the general climate of psychological opinion. It is worth noting that in the early 1970's the idea of purely cognitive biases appeared novel and distinctive, because the prevalence of motivated and emotional biases of judgment was taken for granted by the social psychologists of the time. There followed a period of intense emphasis on cognitive processes, in psychology generally and in the field of judgment in particular. It took another thirty years to achieve what now appears to be a more integrated view of the role of affect in intuitive judgment. [Kahneman, 2002, pp. 470–471]

Heuristics can also be defined as a simple algorithm that, on the basis of a limited amount of information and with the use of rules for concluding a search (both for possible alternatives and for further cues), leads to a decision in short and acceptable periods of time with respect to the demands presented by the environment in which one is working. In an essay published a few years ago Gigerenzer and Selten [2001] relate the example of two teams given the task of constructing a robot able to catch a ball in flight during a game of baseball (the ball could arrive only head on or from behind, but never from the right or from the left). The first team operated on the basis of the principles of classical physics, and on the idea that the robot was a classical reasoner. The team programmed the robot's "mind" with all of the differential and algebraic equations necessary for describing the trajectory of the ball in the real system represented by the earth's surface and the influences owing to air resistance and turbulence. For these reasons the team had to equip the robot with sensors able to grasp the physical factors necessary for the solution of the algebraic-differential system of equations. For example, the robot had to measure the position, the velocity and the departure direction of the ball, its angular movement, the velocity and the direction of the wind, and also the temperature, the air humidity and everything else that was important in the solution of a system of equations. Once the important physical data had been obtained from the environment, the robot, equipped with a physical-mathematical model, had to calculate the trajectory of the ball and where it would fall. Once that point was established the robot then had to move itself in that direction in order to catch the ball in flight. This example shows two important elements: (1) the robot, tied up in its calculations, never caught the ball, because the ball hit the ground well before the robot succeeded in determining the exact point towards which it should move; (2) in analogous situations, one simply does not reason in such a way.

On the other hand, the second team, working with knowledge of the principle of *bounded rationality*, did not program the robot according to a physical-mathematical model, but instead sought a particular piece of environmental data, a cue, a simple measurement, that was correlated with the trajectory of the ball and with its landing point: for example, the angle formed with respect to the ground from the straight line that linked the robot's gaze to the ball was a function of the position of the ball at every moment. Therefore, the robot could make small movements and rapidly assess in this way, at every moment, the new angle, and modifying, if necessary, its own course in order to keep the angle constant. In such a way, the robot had to pay attention to only one piece of data, without the necessity of acquiring other information from its environment or of carrying out complex calculations on that information. In the end the robot succeeded in catching the ball "in flight", without having calculated beforehand the point of impact, but by using one piece of data to guide itself to the right place at the right time [Gigerenzer and Selten, 2001].

## Satisfaction and adaptation

In our lives we often pursue incompatible objectives of different natures. Incompatible objectives are those which cannot be maximized simultaneously: that is to say, the choice which optimizes one of these does not coincide with the choice that would optimize other ones. Therefore, in pursuing multiple objectives a sort of mediation between the different levels of satisfaction to which one aspires is necessary. In other words, an individual, in interacting with the environment, is able to adapt his or her aspiration for each of the objectives that is being pursued. If an objective appears easily reachable, the aspiration level can be raised; if instead the individual encounters difficulty he or she can reduce his/her demands and lower the aspiration level. Therefore, aspiration levels are not static, but are modulated dynamically according to the situation.

Selten [1998] returned to this idea in order to formulate a model that shows that it is possible to construct a theory of *bounded rationality* in which the behaviour is non-optimizing, but not irrational. In fact, because of the proven adaptive value of the forms of reasoning which determine human behaviour, that behaviour, even though in many situations it does not follow the rules of logical inference, cannot be considered irrational. According to Selten the theory of aspiration adaptation is rational because it is based on reasonable systematic procedures. The central elements of his theory are: a) a *table of influence*, which describes the expectations and the causal effects; and b) an *aspiration adaptation table*, which guides the search for alternatives and their selection. Without entering into the mathematical details of the theory, one can say that it contemplates a series of objectives that are incompatible but simultaneously pursued. No function succeeds in managing the optimization of all of the objectives at the same time. A multi-level optimization would in fact be necessary, while an adaptation of aspirations succeeds in overcoming the difficulties presented by the pursuit and comparison of heterogeneous objectives [Selten and Selten, 1988]. It must be said that each objective has an associated hierarchy of aspiration values. The sum of aspirations at any given moment is called the *level of aspiration*, namely the level we would like to reach at a certain moment by means of a certain action, even if at that moment the objectives do not have a value which coincides with those aspirations. In order to modify the existing values of each objective (and, consequently, the level of aspiration), all the values for all of the objectives have to be above (or at least equal to) the relative level of aspiration, therefore making action necessary. It is this action which makes the values of the objectives and of the relative aspirations gradually come together to meet each other, so to speak, one at a time. Selten defined the interactions that modify the value of one single objective at a time as "atomistic". It is conceivable that the decision maker also nurtures expectations on the influence exercised by each action on the various objectives. On a formal level this is expressed by a table of influence that specifies the qualitative effect of an action on each objective.

Aspiration adaptation takes place, therefore, on a single objective at a time. Given the available actions, the adaptation consists of seeing how far the improvement of the existing level of aspiration can be pushed. The objectives are ordered according to their urgency and the aspiration growth respects this order (the first variable is called the *most urgent variable*). Analogously, when it is not possible to achieve an objective there is the possibility to withdraw (the *withdrawal variable*). An important aspect is that both of these factors (the *urgency variable* and *the withdrawal variable*) depend on the aspiration level. Thus, an aspiration adaptation table has the following components:

- the objectives (or better, the variable-objectives, assuming that a value can be associated to the objectives);
- the scale of aspiration values for each objective;
- the order of priority of each aspiration level;
- the objective on which to carry out a withdrawal for each aspiration level.

How can we describe, then, the decision making process in light of the aspiration adaptation model? It would be too complex to examine it in detail. Nevertheless, a simplified description can be useful for understanding how this process can occur in the domain of *bounded rationality*. Generally speaking, one assumes that the decision maker knows the aspiration levels attainable through the group of alternatives within which he/she may choose. The sum of these states constitutes a *set of feasibilities* [Selten, 2001]. In a sort of ideal graphic one could start from an initial point in order to then navigate within the aspiration adaptation table, following as much as possible an upwards direction within the area demarcating the viable levels. This can improve the adaptation level for all of the variables, but can also require, for some of these, a decrease in the aspiration level. This is characteristic of a system in which the objectives are asymmetrical, that is of a system in which the objectives cannot be optimized together.

According to Selten's perspective the *aspiration level* plays a different role from that played by the *satisfaction process* in Simon's theory (in which the decision maker immediately notices if an alternative meets or does not meet a certain level of aspiration). Selten's decision maker does not know the consequences of a certain action, but he/she considers the possible effects of it, letting him/herself be guided by qualitative assessments. In the case of variable-objectives correlated with risk, Selten maintains that risk and uncertainty are not distinct, because risk is tied to assessments of probability. The variable-objectives correlated with risks are used in order to reduce the negative effects in the event that these should occur (consider, for example, the money put aside by a bank in order to face the risks of a financial crisis). It is however clear that the higher the number of variables, the less the risk, and this is the case especially when the probability assessments of the risks are difficult.

The aspiration levels have to be such that they allow the decision maker to verify whether or not they have been reached, at least after the consequences of the decision have become clear. The same variable-objectives correlated with risk must comply with this criterion. Naturally, these aspiration levels have a conventional nature and the significance required in empirical research is different in different fields [Selten 1991]. In this sense, the aspiration levels are not the result of an individual adaptation, but rather of a social process. Selten also analyzes the possible modifications to the theory suggested by experimental evidence. Among these modifications, one of the most important is a more in-depth theory on the formation of quantitative expectations. Another modification concerns an adjustment to the aspiration adaptation table. Decision makers, Selten maintains, do not always know what they want. In new situations, objectives have to be formulated. Where does the aspiration table originate from? Only a finite number of decision-making alternatives can be considered, even if generally speaking there are an infinite number of alternatives. How is this selection made? In other words, how are quantitative or qualitative expectations on the variable-objectives formulated? The aspiration adaptation theory leaves the objective-formation process largely un-modelled [Selten, 1998].

In Selten's account the main characteristics of *bounded rationality* are the following:

(a)  incomparability of objectives;
(b)  situational procedural preferences;
(c)  decisions based on qualitative expectations;
(d)  objective variables correlated with risk;
(e)  cautious optimism in the search for alternatives and in the use of qualitative expectations;
(f)  integrated decisions on the decision-making resources.

The first four characteristics have already been considered. With regards to "cautious optimism", it must be said that in further developments of the theory, the states that are only potentially feasible are also considered. Only full-blown impracticability is a motive for rejection towards the lower end of the aspiration level (in the example above, the *set of feasibilities* included only the levels considered to be assuredly feasible). This optimism is, however, tempered by a principle of caution which counsels not proceeding if the level of feasibility is no higher than "potential". Finally, the description "integrated decisions" refers to the fact that the theory simultaneously pertains to decisions among the alternatives and to decisions about the resources to be used in order to carry the decision-making process forward.

## A critique of classical economic rationality

As previously stated, the idea at the basis of Kahneman and Tversky's program is that the application of heuristics is due mainly to the existence of constraints — already indicated by Simon during the mid-1950s — which impede the application of more "rational" or thorough analyses: pressure in terms of time, the unavailability of all of the relevant information, uncertainty, badly defined objectives, changing conditions, memory limitations, cognitive limitations for the processing of information, and so on. The use of these heuristics has for the most part been considered a sort of defect, a defect which can be remedied only when one has the necessary means at one's disposal. These heuristics (with the *biases* that result from them) are considered to be "non-adaptive" and potentially harmful. In considering the asymmetries between classical norms and effective reasoning as errors, the "heuristics and *biases*" program shares a common outlook with the classical approach, which sees in statistical tools a model of reasoning and of decision making that is both normative and descriptive [Gigerenzer and Goldstein, 1996].

In much analysis of the decision making process the idea persists that there exists, after all, a normative reference or an ideal to which we can aspire, and one that we can reach once all of the constraints that condition us are eliminated. This is what Gary Klein defines as the *gold standard* of decision making [Klein, 1998], which consists precisely in maximizing the expected utility or in optimizing the result by choosing, among the possible alternatives, the one that provides the best overall result. There is, then, an optimal result that could be known to all through the use of powerful scientific instruments developed for that purpose. The application of heuristics is therefore a consequence of our own limitations. In fact in 1955 Herbert Simon had already contrasted satisfaction with optimization. Searching for satisfaction, rather than optimization, means choosing, among the possible alternatives, the one that satisfies a certain level of expectation, which is the only way of facing the limitations of time, of knowledge and of our own computational ability. It is in this way that we settle for something that is less than optimal in order to find a solution within the period of time and using the means made possible by the circumstances and by the environment. The *heuristic of satisfaction* allows individuals to compensate for their own limited abilities in terms of finding, memorizing, and analysing information.

The question of whether it is possible to optimize a decision — that is, whether or not an optimal level exists that one can realistically aspire to (or whether this level is reachable within a time period and with tools of a capacity that is not infinite); or whether every decision made in the real world must necessarily be subject to some form of compromise in order to be made — is of crucial importance. In fact, demonstrating definitively that optimization is an unrealistic objective would move the focus of studies on decision making towards the search for ways in which one can make a decision that is pragmatically the best for everyone; or satisfactory for all with respect to the aspiration levels of each person.

This subject is of great relevance because despite the discoveries of the last decades, modern economic theory is still based on an unrealistic representation of decision making, which portrays economic agents as fully rational Bayesian maximizors of subjective utility [Selten, 2001]. Simon had for some time grasped the theoretical and empirical abstractness and implausibility of a model of *homo economicus* characterized by a knowledge of the important aspects of his/her environment which is, if not complete, at least clear and substantial; by a stable and well-organized system of preferences; and by a calculation ability that would allow the individual to determine which actions should enable him/her to reach the highest possible point in his/her personal scale of preferences [Simon, 1957].

Already in the mid 1900s empirical results and theoretical developments had raised doubts about this model of *homo economicus*. For this reason, Simon proposed to replace the ideal decision maker's "Olympic rationality" with a type of rational behaviour compatible with the access to information and computational capacities actually possessed by human beings, in the typical environments in which they live. It must be said that doubt had also been cast on the theory that decision making based on the principle of the maximization of expected utility is a normative and descriptive principle of human behaviour, by a few paradoxes that result from this theory, the most famous of which was demonstrated in the early 1960s, by the American physicist William Newcomb, and taken up again a few years later by Robert Nozick [1985, 1993]. In light of these and other problems with the theory, must one modify the principle of the maximization of expected utility or completely give up on it, admitting that people who are inexpert in statistics, when facing everyday situations, adopt quite different strategies to optimize their choices?

The concept of *bounded rationality* — which still today has not been fully elaborated — has been used in a variety of ways by various researchers over the years, and in ways not always corresponding to the intentions of its creator. Perhaps in order to explain exactly what *bounded rationality* is, it is best to begin by explaining what it is not. Some authors have used this term in reference to *bounded optimization* [Sargent, 1993]: that is to say, optimization that takes into account the costs of the search for information and for possible alternatives, and also of the costs of the determination of the optimal process (in that regard, the risk of an infinite regression presented by the adoption of this method has already been mentioned). This model also appears unrealistic because of the volume of calculations and the quantity of knowledge that it requires. In this sense, optimization in bounded conditions does not correspond with a paradigm of *bounded rationality*.

In our exposition of the various theories of rationality we have moved further and further away from the idea that the functioning of the human mind is guided by logical-formal norms. The departure from these norms has historically been interpreted as a sort of recurring fallacy, and therefore, as a reflex, *bounded rationality* has been interpreted as synonymous with a limitation of reason, as though there existed an ideal reason and rationality which could be used as a standard of reference. This point of view does not take into account the environmental dimension, which has been highlighted by Simon. It does not make sense, in fact, to speak of an abstract rationality, divorced from the context in which it operates. In evaluating the rationality of a certain behaviour one must consider — as Simon made clear — both blades of the scissors: not only the cognitive limitations, but also the constraints and the demands that derive from the environment. In our habitual lines of reasoning we set a limit on the search for both possible alternatives among which to choose, and on the pathways of the decision; moreover, we follow more adaptive objectives such as the satisfaction of specific levels of aspiration concerning our objectives and needs; finally, we adapt our aspirations to the circumstances in order to reach a satisfactory compromise. Schematizing, the models of *bounded rationality* proposed up to this point include simple rules for the *search* (for alternatives and cues), for the *conclusion of the search* (for example, when a level of aspiration is met), and for the *making of a decision* (for example, the object favoured by the most persuasive line of reasoning).

Recently, Gigerenzer and his collaborators have taken up the concept of *limited rationality* again, re-evaluating one of the two blades of Simon's scissors that had been neglected until that time: the blade pertaining to environmental constraints. Gigerenzer designed a program for re-evaluating the importance of the environment in promoting the evolution of heuristics that respond adaptively to environmental challenges (from which comes the notion of "ecological rationality"). In *Simple Heuristics That Make us Smart* [1999], he proposed a *second probabilistic revolution* that would substitute the image of an omniscient mind with the more realistic image of a limited mind, which would however be able to draw on a "tool box" equipped with strategies that would enable us to efficiently face situations of uncertainty [Morini, 2003, p. xiv]. A characteristic feature of these heuristics is that they are based on a single reason [Gigerenzer and Goldstein, 1996]. That is, they are non-compensatory strategies, strategies which cannot be integrated with the available information. Evans and Over [1997] identified two different incompatible notions of rationality : the first is represented by cognitive activities (language, reasoning, decision making, etc.) directed at a general dependability and efficiency and at the reaching of objectives; and the second relates to the afore-mentioned activities when an individual has a reason for what he/she is doing, ratified by a normative theory [Chater et al., 2003].

Gigerenzer's arguments are based on the two aspects already pointed out by Simon: the presence of cognitive limitations and the importance of the environment, to which he added the experimental evidence that suggests that in realistic situations some simple heuristics (such as the one called *take the best*) perform better than (or at least as well as) sophisticated algorithms such as linear regression or Bayes's theorem.

## A critique of constructivism and evolutionary rationality

The development of a strict theory of utility in choices made in conditions of risk or uncertainty followed from the pioneering work of the mathematician von Neumann and of the economist Morgenstern. In the *Theory of Games and Economic Behaviour* [1944] — a book that influenced the intellectual development of generations of economists — these authors demonstrated the existence of a *function of utility* able to provide a prescriptive perspective for the analysis of risky behaviour, describing in addition a decision-making path that follows a clear table of preferences in which the best choice is that which always maximizes the *expected utility*.

This model has four main characteristics:

- a cardinal utility function;
- a complete group of alternative strategies;
- a distribution of probabilities of future scenarios linked to each alternative;
- a policy of the maximization of expected utility

According to the normative model, a decision is *rational* when it is stamped by formal criteria and by coherence expressed through a sequence of axiomatic demonstrations that represent not just a model, but a true paradigm [Hogart and Reder, 1986]. Among the axioms at the basis of the *theory of expected utility* there are:

(a) *Axiom of transitivity*: if result A is preferred to result B, and result B is preferred to result C, then result A must be preferred to result C;

(b) *Axiom of dominance*: if option A is more advantageous than option B in all of the possible configurations, then one must prefer option A to option B regardless of the present configuration;

(c) *Axiom of invariance*: the order of the preferences cannot be modified or overturned because of the effect of the way in which the options are proposed. In other words, the decision should be insensitive to the variations in the presentation of the decision-making problem.

Furthermore, individual maximization of the *expected utility* represents a normative criterion for describing the ideal approach of an economic agent who must decide among risky alternatives. In such a case, the approach of the decision-maker will be one of neutrality, aversion or inclination towards risk. Nonetheless, even while being mostly in keeping with the rational behaviour postulated by the normative theories, the aversion-to-risk approach does not constitute the rule (as the work of Kahneman and Tversky will show), because if it did, widespread phenomena such as gambling, in which the agents engage in and even seek opportunities for risky behaviours, could not be explained.

More generally speaking, while the research of Neumann and Morgenstern encouraged experimental research in the fields of economy and psychology through the verification of the descriptive validity of the axioms [McFadden, 2005], they also established the bases of the modern *game theory* (a mathematical theory that analyzes individual decisions in situations of *strategic interaction*), according to which a subject's decisions inevitably influence, through the dynamics of retroaction, the results attainable from a hypothetical adversary [Aliprantis and Chakrabarti, 2000]. The attempt to construct strict mathematical models has as its objective the analysis of the strategies available to the individual players and the evaluation of the probability of the events, which obviously depend on the choices of the adversaries [Lucchetti, 2008]. Through the mathematical axioms postulated by the *model of expected utility*, *game theory* has been applied to the most diverse decision-making contexts — from economic to military, and from political to psychological and social — giving rise to fertile trans-disciplinary research programs, as the Nobel prize for economics of 1994 illustrates: it was awarded to John Nash, John Harsanyi and Reinhard Selten.

It must be said that the tendency of neoclassical economic theory to adopt mechanistic models has not only had the effect of progressively downgrading the concepts of *choice* and *decision making* to mere *problem solving*, but also that of segregating them to a misunderstood methodological value-neutrality: in the end these theories lack explanatory conviction, as they are distant from the real dynamics of human behaviour. Describing the decision-making process and human reasoning through the formula of the *maximization of expected utility* is like describing a complex physical system with a simple formula. The variables in play are so numerous and based on so few verifiable and measurable dimensions as to render the attempt completely irrelevant.

In his article "Economics and Knowledge" [1937], Friedrich von Hayek — one of the most influential exponents of the Austrian School and a Nobel prize winner for economics in 1974 — embarked on a theoretical path away from the neoclassical concept of *equilibrium*, favouring the passage from an abstract rationality to a rationality founded on a conscious fallibility of human knowledge and on the dynamism of individual action. Hayek's *evolutionistic rationalism* is a radical critique of classical rationality, whose roots lie completely in Cartesian constructivism. In *Studies in Philosophy, Politics and Economics* he explains:

> Descartes maintained that all of the useful human institutions were, and should be, the deliberate creation of conscious reason ( . . . ) an ability of the mind to arrive at the truth through a deductive process of few obvious and indubitable premises. [1967, p. 85]

According to Hayek human beings are not only incapable of arriving at truth through logical-formal deductions, but also of mastering their own destinies: "( . . . ) the individual's same reason is always progressing, bringing him/her towards the unknown and the unexpected, where he/she learns new things" [Hayek, 1994, p. 559]. Hayek's critique of constructivism rests on the idea of autonomy of the economy with respect to the exact sciences. Economic phenomena — fed as they are by unforeseen changes produced by complex individual interactions — prove to be irreducible to operationalism or to deductive inferences. From Hayek's perspective human action is unforetellable, and thus his conclusions are closely related to the theory of the *heterogenesis of ends*, according to which human actions often lead to ends different from those that were anticipated beforehand. Human reason should therefore recognize its own limits and consider the fact that a *spontaneous order* — that is to say, an order generated without any design — can by far exceed the projects that human beings create through deliberate plans [Hayek, 1988]. It follows that an economic decision never emerges from given alternatives, but from a process of individual creation and elaboration external to every programmatic deliberation [Hayek, 1952]. The theory is based on an appreciation of the incompleteness and the fallibility of human knowledge, and on the awareness that the value of objects is not intrinsic and self-evident, but subjectively attributed by individuals. Abstract rationalism demands that agents possess a complete set of information on the advantages and disadvantages of each choice, more information than a human mind could ever retain or process [McFadden, Smith and Kahneman, 2005]. A similar omniscience would, however, transform economics

> ( . . . ) into a branch of pure logic, that is to say into a sum of self-evident propositions that, on par with mathematics and geometry, are subject to no other test than that of internal coherence. [Hayek, 1967/1998, p. 229]

Borrowing the concepts of evolution and of the *spontaneous order* of society and of institutions from Bernard Mandeville's book *The fable of the bees* [1714], Hayek re-proposes the idea that individual actions, however much driven by selfish objectives, have positive consequences for the community. In *The Sensory Order* [1952], the strong psychological component of Hayekian individualism reveals itself in all its clarity. This famous study, which can be counted among the original approaches of cognitive psychology to the theory of classical economics [Rizello, 1997], bears the unmistakable character of individualistic psychology. Hayek is convinced that in order to understand the dynamics of individual choices it is necessary to probe the limits of the mind, taking neurophysiologic and psychological evidence into consideration. Anticipating in some ways the great era of the neurosciences [Fuster, 1997; Paller, 2001] he seeks to trace the qualitative dimensions of perception back to the activity of the brain, analyzing in particular the process that allows for the transformation of these dimensions into personal knowledge. The human mind, he observed, is a *framework* containing a set of guiding *patterns* that, on the basis of previous experiences, order our vision of the world, slowly but relentlessly carrying out continuous adjustments in response to environmental stimuli.
According to Hayek, that which

> we call "mind" is thus a particular order of a set of events taking place in some organism and in some manner related to but not identical with, the physical order of events in the environment. [1963, p. 16]

This group of events — regulated by selective and creative competitions internal to the brain, successively transformed into epigenetic marks inside of a *frame* characteristic of the species — subjects the sensorial *inputs* to a continuous remodelling on the basis of meta-conscious and pre-sensorial dynamics, an effect of both subjective experiences, and of neuronal connections: dynamics that, having settled themselves over the course of individual history through organic links with the physical, social and cultural environment, further the biological evolution of the species.

Thanks to modern studies of the human nervous system, we know that neural circuits and cerebral structures, designed to interact with the external reality, are continuously modified, evolving in directions neither foreseeable nor predetermined. The brain is the residence of an implicit and subconscious knowledge which is situated above the level traditionally assigned to what we usually think of as knowledge; it is clear and deliberate and cannot be known, because it is too elevated for the human mind. Information based on external data becomes knowledge through an endogenous and subjective *process* [Rizello, 1995].

Individual action appears, therefore, to be the result of two forms of knowledge: one conscious and the other subconscious. For this reason the decision maker will have to face a complex set of factors which cannot be encompassed by the rigid structures of traditional logic, inevitably making errors in judgement that are often very significant. While classical economists attribute the imperfect interpretation of external signals to individual errors, Hayek ascribes these same errors to the ways in which knowledge is constructed. In fact, if it is true that individuals receive or acquire information, it is also true that they operate on the basis of a knowledge that is the result of the elaboration — through tacit, personal and often idiosyncratic mechanisms — of that same information. What Hayek is describing is a strongly *path-dependant* process of knowledge formation [Pierson, 1993], because it is conditioned by the history, by the genetic characteristics and above all by the experience, conscious and subconscious, of each and every single individual. It is this idea that pushes Hayek to maintain that

> human decisions must always appear as the result of the whole of a human personality — that means the whole of a person's mind — which, as we have seen, we cannot reduce to something else. [1963, p. 193]

The empirical and predictive fragility of normative theories with respect to real decision-making dynamics became clearer and clearer in the second half of the twentieth century. The ideal of "Olympic" rationality, worthy of the Platonic "Sky of Ideas," according to the ironic words of Simon [1988], fell into disfavour because of substantial difficulties which make its application to everyday decision-making contexts and to real behaviour impossible. Although consumer conditioning generates market behaviour that is in many cases close to the conventional model, when we ask consumers direct or unusual questions regarding beliefs or values, a strong departure from the conventional rationalist models of the economists can be noted [McFadden, 2005].

## Substantive rationality *versus* procedural rationality

In fact we may suggest that a large part of Simon's philosophy consists of the investigation of the limits of human nature. His descriptive approach to the study of decisions of the *grounded-in-reality* type is born of observation and not of axioms or principles and enunciations made beforehand [Berthoz, 2004]. So-called *behavioral economics*, which originate in the studies of Simon, attempt to integrate the classical theory of rational choice with new hypotheses borrowed from experimental psychology, moving the focus from *substantive rationality* to *procedural rationality*. In the cognitive approach the concept of decision making is not limited to the choice itself, but includes the definition of the problem, the processing of information, the identification of alternatives, their assessment, and finally a choice [Codara, 1998]. The objective is to increase the explicative and predictive power of economics by placing it on a more realistic basis, with the conviction that by incorporating the dynamics of individual decisions into economic theory it would be possible to generate new and more plausible theoretical models [Motterlini and Piattelli Palmarini, 2005]. Bounded rationality proposes a *heuristic-adaptive* model of rational choice in contrast with the neo-classical *logical-deductive* one.

Simon thus explains the limits of neo-classical economic theory:

> The classical model requires the knowledge of all of the choice alternatives available; it requires the complete knowledge of the consequences of each alternative, or the possibility of calculating them; it requires certainty in the present and future assessment of such consequences by the decision maker; it requires the ability to compare the consequences among themselves, regardless of how varied and heterogeneous they may be, in terms of some coherent measurement of utility. [1985, p. 295]

The inaccessibility of all of the information required, the impossibility of predicting the consequences of each hypothetical action, and the unavoidable cognitive-computational limits of individuals bring the very concept of rationality back into question, with the consequent shift from the criterion of optimization to that of satisfaction (*satisficing*) in the choice among alternatives [Simon, 1987]. That is to say, an alternative is satisfactory if a series of criteria exist that describe the alternatives of minimum satisfaction and if this alternative corresponds to such criteria or surpasses them [March and Simon, 1958/66]. Therefore, the key words in the "bounded rationality" decision-making process are *searching* and *satisfaction*. In conditions of uncertainty — conditions in which the search for solutions is rather costly — the *homo economicus* would accept solutions that are "good enough", stopping at the one that satisfies most criteria rather than seeking the optimal solution at any cost [Berthoz, 2004]. In this sense, a theory of bounded rationality must first and foremost contemplate a *theory of search* [March, 1994] which does not conform to the normative rule for when to stop — according to which the search for alternatives ends only when one reaches an ideal optimizing result — but instead concentrates on personal *levels of aspiration* [Simon, 1957]. In other words, the search for alternatives ends with the alternative that, according to the circumstances, most satisfies our needs and objectives. Simon's model, inspired by a *procedural* version of rationality [Simon, 1978], allows for the identification of at least three sources of endogenous change in the decision-making process:

(a) a cognitive representation of knowledge, which can vary from one decision maker to another and in the different phases of the decision-making process;
(b) a structuring of the objectives, which are not known beforehand, but rather are formulated during the decision-making process
(c) criteria for the termination of the search, according to which the decision maker stops his/her search at the first satisfactory solution, rather than investing further energy and resources in looking for a better solution [Simon, 1985].

In spite of its theoretical and empirical scope, the concept of *bounded rationality* has been contested by some scholars, who argue that the adoption of this term would entail the existence of an *unbounded rationality* in the neoclassical model of rationality. To such an objection one could respond in the manner of Selten, who writes that it is possible "to construct theories of bounded rationality in which behaviour is non-optimizing but not irrational" [Selten, 1998, p. 192]. This is because at the basis of the theory of *bounded rationality* is the idea that a human being's behaviour does not follow logical-formal rules. Nonetheless, because of the high adaptive value of the forms of reasoning that determine this behaviour, it cannot be considered irrational. Simon's objective is to show the invalidity of an "abstract rationality" that ignores both the limits imposed by the external environment (*task environment*) as well as the imperfect cognitive structure of human beings [Simon, 1990]. The ability of the human mind to solve complex problems is very limited in comparison with the number of such problems that must be faced and solved [Rumiati and Bonini, 1992]. The real world is, in fact, composed of a sum of chaotic and ambiguous data that are irreducible to logical-deductive inferences. Taking action, therefore, means dealing with incomplete information, time constraints, and restricted computational abilities. The attention that has been dedicated to the decision-making process, rather than to the choice itself, has opened a path for the study of the procedures by which decision makers acquire information about the world around them, re-work this information and, finally, use this information in order to formulate their choices.

## The adaptive decision maker

Experimental evidence has shown that, in the act of making a decision, a large number of individuals take what can accurately be called mental "short-cuts" which are easy and fallacious at the same time, and which above all cannot be traced to simple equations [Piattelli Palmarini, 1993]. In human action, that is to say, the algorithmic inference schemas of deductive theories prove to be ineffective. In fact, while they produce coherent results when applied correctly, they nevertheless appear to be slow for the cognitive work and for the magnitude of the memory space required. Contrarily, a heuristic grid that filters decisions spares the subjects from calculations that are too long and that would make human reasoning completely inefficient. These are real behavioural stratagems that are compatible with the difficulty of the task and introduce great savings into decision-making processes. However, exactly because they shorten and simplify our reasoning processes, they are the cause of self-deceptions and perceptive *biases* and lead our reasoning towards gross, systematic, and persistent failures. In this sense, knowing the heuristics and the potential *biases* in play means understanding the ways in which we respond to environmental issues in accordance with our cognitive system. There is yet another limit that any attempt at decision-making optimization must face: the fact that the process is not able to optimize itself or its own procedures. The rules of optimization are not able to explain and justify the search for the information necessary to the making of a decision. "The attempt at such a justification would in fact involve us in an infinite backwards logical process, in which each proposition would be just as arbitrary as the one that precedes it" [Simon, 1988, p. 36]. As previously observed, Gigerenzer [2001] pointed out, especially in *real-world* problems, some arguments in defence of such a description of decision-making in terms of heuristics. His objective is to broaden research on the decision-making process with regard to both the biological and the psychological dimensions of the mind. Our model of the mind, from omniscient (as in the case of Laplace's famous "demon" which could carry out complex Bayesian calculations) must become limited and adaptive in order to effectively face situations of uncertainty. In the second half of twentieth century psychological research showed how the ideal *homo economicus*, when faced with the real behaviour of the decision maker of normative-descriptive theories, is as theoretically strong as it is empirically vulnerable [McFadden, 2005]. The new model of the decision-making process would be characterized by the idea that behaviour is local, adaptive, changeable, learned, dependent upon the context and influenced by the complex interactions of perceptions, motivations, attitudes, and affections. The model of the adaptive *decision maker* fine-tuned by Payne, Bettman and Johnson [1993] reveals, in fact, how the same individual can often use different strategies for the simplification of information [Braun and Yaniv, 1992] based on a number of factors: the way in which the information is presented, the nature of the response, the complexity of the problem, and the decision-making context. Such variables, regardless of the values of the alternatives, influence the selection of strategies, modifying the cognitive effort necessary in order to implement them [Bettman, 1993]. It is on the strength of this insight that the process of choice has been considered to be a highly contingent form of information processing, a form in which individuals use multiple and distinct strategies that include choices based on heuristics as an adaptive response to individuals' limited ability in information processing and to the complexity of decision-making tasks [Payne, Bettman and Johnson, 1993]. The sum of the evidence discussed renders an *evolutionistic model of rationality* plausible, a model that, if not to explain the precise nature of the rational process, certainly indicates the direction towards which it tends. There are not, in fact, plausible reasons for believing that each and every thing is inclined towards a final optimal state, but there are good reasons to conclude that there is "a constant movement towards an objective that is itself continuously in movement" [Simon, 1988, p. 111].

## Emotional intelligence and the affect heuristic

Human beings very frequently act on the basis of automatic mental processes, often subconscious, independent of volition and intuitive, or simply on the basis of common sense. In general, a large part of the success of a decision is due to good intuitive faculties. In contrast to ordinary sensorial perception and logical reasoning, intuitions often presents themselves to us through sudden illuminations. It is not uncommon, in the history of science, for inventors, scientists and researchers to have conceived their ideas or hypotheses following dreams, sudden "brainwaves" or irrational and non-analytic reflections. One needs only think of the falling apple that led Newton to the discovery of the law of gravity, or of the lamp swaying back and forth in the cathedral of Pisa that inspired Galileo to "see" the rule of oscillation of the pendulum.

Some ideas, points of view and interpretations of data first reach the mind by way of intuition because they are based on a sum of more "accessible" knowledge. In this sense intuition — which is a constant factor in reasoning — is not influenced by uncertainty. Reasoning comes into play (when it comes into play) only afterwards, in making explicit the options among which to choose . It is here that doubt (also a constant factor in reasoning) emerges, which leads to the formulation of incompatible thoughts about the same mental object. Intuition and reasoning are separate cognitive processes, both by now well described in the psychological literature. Intuition is usually the first cognitive process used, but significant errors of assessment are often attributable to the process. Intuition is a rapid associative mechanism, automatic, and generating results almost immediately, that does not require any particular effort and produces results which are difficult to verify. Reasoning is slower, serial, controlled, flexible, and is also exposed to the risk of errors. Logic and intuition have equal roles in the functioning of the human mind and both respond to the demands of cognitive economies. Thus there is no need to be trapped in the false dilemma between those who maintain that the dominant component of human cognitive processes is logic (and not heuristics, because of their potentially *bias*-generating nature); and those who, on the contrary, maintain that heuristics are the dominant component of human cognitive processes (and not logic, because the majority of our cognitive processes are not of a computational type).

For much of the twentieth century error was considered to be only a clouding of reason, but it has recently emerged as a subject for independent study, a constant part of human reasoning determined by factors such as:

(a) quantity or quality of the information;
(b) selective attention;
(c) limited memory;
(d) emotion; and
(e) limited cognitive capacities.

Through research into and analysis of individual behaviours the *psychology of decision making* has provided a growing body of experimental evidence over the past few decades [Piattelli Palmarini, 2005]. This evidence suggests not only that error and uncertainty are inherent to the decision-making process (and, more generally, to the functioning of the mind), but also that sentiments, values and emotions are as well. Previously, the exaltation of rationality had allowed us to believe

( . . . ) that decision making was the product of reasoning. That it was the privilege of human beings and of the structures of our brains situated in the frontal lobe, as with big corporations, where the offices of the people who make the decisions are situated at the top of skyscrapers. [Berthoz, 2004, p. 4]

In some cases the attempt to identify the sources of certain rational knowledge conceals an *authoritative* notion of knowledge suffused with the belief in a transcendental entity (God, nature, or that same rationality) which is in itself an origin of certainties. In *Conjectures and Refutations; The Growth of Scientific Knowledge*, Popper explains:

> Every solution of a problem raises new unsolved problems; the more so the deeper the original problem and the bolder its solution. The more we learn about the world, and the deeper our learning, the more conscious, specific, and articulate will be our knowledge of what we do not know, our knowledge of our ignorance. For this, indeed, is the main source of our ignorance — the fact that our knowledge can be only finite, while our ignorance must necessarily be infinite. [Popper, 1963, p. 28]

The distinguished philosopher proposes the model of a *contextual rationality* that regulates individual behaviour according to the context in which the individual finds him/herself. In his opinion, assigning a higher position to logic with respect to empirics would mean choosing the dogmatism of a system of rules closed in on itself, completely impermeable to experience. It is not without significance that the term "rationalization" was adopted in psychoanalysis in order to designate the tendency of neurotic individuals to provide rational explanations intended to justify attitudes, opinions and behaviours that would otherwise be unacceptable: dynamics which are typical of the instinctual sphere, but that in this case are caught up in a closed explanatory system devoid of any connection with reality, although equipped with a logic of their own.

The countless paradoxes in normative theories that emerged starting in the 1950s [Allais, 1953; Ellsberg, 1961], together with an ample harvest of experimental studies on human reasoning and decision making [Kahneman and Tversky, 2000] indicate that the above-mentioned "deviations" represent natural dynamics of cognitive processes and that the errors that we make in decisions and in reasoning are inevitable products of the human mind, an expression that is to say of a sort of *rational ignorance* [Downs, 1957]. The attempt to interpret these limits produced many studies. Starting in 1968 in particular, the research of Kahneman and Tversky showed that the "Olympic" rationality postulated by *rational choice* is empirically untenable.

The credit undoubtedly goes to Kahneman for having shed light on the very close relationship between psychology and economics, especially with regards to judgement and decision making in conditions of uncertainty. In situations of risk and uncertainty, in fact, the normative theories (of "sensible", "planned" and "coherent" behaviour) lose their effectiveness, because they consider it impossible that a choice can have a solution that is not optimal. This study enthused and at the same time dismayed economists who found themselves in the position as people who "( . . . ) stand watching the carpenters while they construct the scaffold for their hanging" [McFadden, 2005, p. 35].

Studies of economic psychology have highlighted the fact that the success or failure of decision makers depends on processes that are much more complex than the mere differences in efficiency postulated by classical economic theory. In reality, *homo economicus*, that is to say the maximizor of stable preferences, is by now an "endangered species" [Motterlini and Piattelli Palmarini, 2005]. In their by now famous book *Choices, Frames and Values* [2000], Kahneman and Tversky provided a good synthesis of the results obtained from the research program known as the *Heuristics and biases approach* [Kahneman, Knetsch and Thaler, 1990], which consists of submitting, in carefully controlled experimental conditions, decision-making problems to sample groups of individuals in order to determine whether these people reason and make decisions according to rational criteria. The many experiments carried out show that the divergences between what was predicted by the model and individuals' real *performances* can be explained by the existence of rational rules and of distorted (*biased*) principles of choice deriving from the interference of cognitive factors and of context relative to the interpretation of the problem and to the available information. One of the most striking results is the so-called *framing effect* [Tversky and Kahneman, 1981], which points out how alternative descriptions of the same decision-making problem can lead to different preferences.

From Tversky and Kahneman's point of view, the value of an alternative cannot be judged in an absolute sense, but only in relation to the context. Losses or earnings have, in fact, a distinct *cognitive* impact on the agent, as they alter the salience of the available information and influence the propensity towards risk [Tversky, Sattah and Slovic, 1988]. In this sense, one can say that the decision-making process is characterized by two phases: *framing* and *assessment*. In the first phase the decision maker "frames" the available options, their possible results, and the respective probabilities in relation to the choices to be made; in the second phase the decision maker gets a sense for the decision-making context, assesses the possible consequences, and finally makes a choice. There is no empirical certainty that the assessment process meets the coherency requirements of rational behaviour. The *frames*, in fact, prompt individuals to use information in the form suggested by the stimulus [Slovic, 1972]; these suggestions may entail that they pay attention only to certain aspects of the alternatives, evaluate the consequences in an incorrect way, and examine only a part of the information in their possession. In other words, it is possible to frame a decision-making task in such a way as to alter the perceived *status quo* and also, therefore, the choice [Tversky and Kahneman, 1981; Sonnemans, Schram and Offerman, 1994].

In 1979, Kahneman and Tversky presented an article entitled "Prospect Theory: An Analysis of Decision under Risk" in the journal *Econometrica*. Because of the innovativeness of their approach, the care with which their experiments were conducted, and their brilliant interpretation of the behavioural data, this article helped change many researchers' opinions on the validity of the classical model's concepts of rationality and maximization. In this article the authors make an accurate and realistic description of individual behaviours under risky circumstances, revealing, through *prospect theory*, the inadequacy of Bernoulli's theorem, but above all showing how human beings are sensitive to differences rather than to absolute values. The limitation of Bernoulli's model is in its proposal of only one continuous utility curve, regardless of the context and of any reference to earnings or losses that are possibly reachable. Individuals, instead, assess the outcomes of a decision on the basis of factors such as the context or the individual's own condition at the moment of decision-making.

Among the main suppositions of *prospect theory* is the axiom that in decision making there is a strong dependence upon the context (*frame dependency*), in the sense that individuals mentally structure the different possibilities that present themselves to them (*editing phase*), perceiving data through a psychological "filter" or, better yet, through an interpretive structure that does not correspond to the criteria of an absolute rationality. Substituting the concept of *utility* for that of *value*, one can observe that economic agents manifest different attitudes when facing earnings and losses (the function is convex for the losses and concave for the earnings). In fact, these economic agents confer a very negative value on the losses (the more one looses, the more desperate one is), while in the case of elevated earnings a positive value is attributed to them, although a maximum level of satisfaction is reached which is unaffected even if earnings continue to climb. Furthermore, the utility function in the domain of losses presents a greater inclination than that of earnings, confirming the principle of *loss aversion* [Kahneman and Tversky, 1979], according to which — the final result being equal — the suffering generated by losses is higher than the pleasure determined by earnings: a sort of *mental accounting* that violates the postulations of neo-classical economic theory and significantly influences our real-life decisions [Thaler, 1991; Shefrin and Thaler, 1992]. For example, in the lottery the regret for marginal losses easily surpasses the happiness deriving from comparable wins, a result that contradicts the implications of the maximization of expected utility.

Through development, revisions and generalizations of *prospect theory* it has been possible to confirm numerous anomalies and incoherencies in decision-making behaviour not traceable to the simple criterion of utility. Using the premises of *prospect theory*, Thaler succeeded in explaining two interesting anomalies not contemplated by economic *rational choice*: the *endowment effect* and the *sunk cost effect* [Thaler, 1990]. In some experimental studies [Thaler and Johnson, 1990; Kahneman, Knetsch and Thaler, 1990] Thaler showed how a subject tends to attribute greater value to a good that he/she possesses than he/she would if he/she did not possess it, and this because of an incorrect perception of the opportunity costs of the possessed good. This phenomenon, called the *endowment effect*, generates a true *status quo bias* [Kahneman, Knetsch and Thaler, 1990]. It follows that the maximum value that one is willing to pay in order to acquire a certain item (*willingness to pay*) is less than the minimum value that one would be willing to accept in the sale of the item (*willingness to accept*). This difference is completely neglected by classical economic theory, according to which the curves of indifference do not consider the endowment of the agent in question. The second phenomenon observed is the *sunk cost effect* [Arkes and Blumer, 1985; Arkes and Anyton, 1999; Sutton, 1991; Thaler, 1985]. Now, although standard economic theory ignores both the costs relative to choices already made (the so-called "sunk costs") as well as their influence on the subsequent choices, it has been shown that in assessing an investment or a project individuals give importance to the resources that are already in use and no longer recoverable, above and beyond the costs and the marginal benefits. The explanation for this is that economic agents are inclined to avoid wastefulness, minimizing in this way the "sunk costs", in line with the principle of *loss aversion*. It follows, therefore, that if the choice made is not the absolute best, it will certainly be the most convenient on the basis of costs in terms of time and of the expected benefits.

A cornerstone of *prospect theory* is the idea that "( . . . ) variations of wealth are the bearers of utility rather than states of wealth" [Kahneman and Tversky, 1979, p. 273]. Their studies directed at explaining the way in which consumers approach problems of choice allowed Kahneman and Tversky to investigate the limitations of calculation and of the processing of information that lead individuals to adopt heuristics which are highly adaptive.

## The return of James

In recent years the role of emotions in the decision-making process has been at the centre of an intense debate. In various important studies, the Portuguese neurologist Antonio Damasio — re-elaborating the reflections of the American philosopher and psychologist William James — highlighted how each day we make decisions based on the push of emotions of which we can be more or less conscious on the level of personal and social consequences. In fact Théodule Ribot, the founder of French psychology, had already pointed out how in the etymology of the term *emotion* (from the Latin *e-movere*) the reference to motion, to movement is evident:

> *Emotion is in the order of feeling the equivalent of perception in the intellectual order*, a complex synthetic state essentially made up of produced or arrested movements, of organic modifications (in circulation, respiration, etc.), of an agreeable or painful or mixed state of consciousness peculiar to each emotion. It is a phenomenon of sudden appearance and limited duration; it is always related to the preservation of the individual or the species directly as regards primitive emotions, indirectly as regards derived emotions. [Ribot, 1911, p. 12]

Emotions are quite different from a physiological disorder or from incongruous conduct, and represent a crucial adaptive component of behaviour, because they pervade the rational sphere, promoting their own "interests" (which are not known beforehand, but rather are generated based on an individual's values) in relation to the structures of meaning of a specific situation [Frank, 1990; Frijda, 1988]. According to *appraisal* theorists such as Lazarus [2001] the cognitive assessment of an emotional piece of data constitutes a crucial point in the emotional and decision-making process: in other words, the same stimulus can be interpreted in different ways and, consequently, arouse different emotions.

> During the deliberation that precedes decision making we evaluate — we appraise — the elements involved. This activity of cognitive appraisal precedes judgement and is for some ( . . . ) essential in the appearance of an emotion. We automatically relate everything that we encounter to our intentions and our goals. Appraisal is a very familiar process that complements perception and produces in us the desire to do something. [Berthoz, 2006, pp. 37–38]

One could reasonably affirm that the interweaving among perception, evaluation and emotion makes emotions "constituent" and cognitive elaborations "determining". Frijda [2000, 1986], and Lazarus [1991] defined emotions as being *evaluative* signals of the state of the mind-body system in relation to the attainment of *goals*. If one accepts this characterisation, a rigid demarcation between emotions and cognition will prove difficult: an emotion is no longer a simple signal, but rather an extremely complex "assessment". Damasio, in every one of his premises and implications, puts the existence of a pure, formal and unconditional rationality into doubt. He refers explicitly to Baruch Spinoza, according to whom bad passions are not to be eliminated by means of reason, but rather to be contrasted with other emotions, stronger and more positive [*Ethics*]. According to Damasio, reason and emotion are not separate spheres: on the contrary, reason is guided by the emotional assessment of the consequences of an action.

> What, then, was Descartes' error? ( . . . .) One might begin with a complaint, and reproach him for having persuaded biologists to adopt, to this day, clockwork mechanics as a model for life processes. But perhaps this would not be quite fair and so one might continue with "I think therefore I am". The statement, perhaps the most famous of the history of philosophy ( . . . ), illustrates precisely the opposite of what I believe to be true about the origins of mind and about the relation between mind and body. It suggests that thinking, and awareness of thinking, are the real substrates of being. And since we know that Descartes imagined thinking as an activity quite separate from the body, it does celebrate the separation of the mind, the "thinking thing" (*res cogitans*), from the nonthinking body, that which has extension and mechanical parts (*res extensa*). [Damasio, 1994, p. 248]

From the time of Descartes to today much progress has been made in understanding the reason-emotion connection. There are by now few scholars who are willing to admit the existence of a mind-body dualism, or that the activity of the mind coincides with pure reasoning and that the activity of the body is set on the satisfaction of physical needs. Such separateness is for the most part a myth. The mind does not move from a disembodied "cogito" to the reign of pure biology. It is not only correlated with the entire organism, but it constitutes a unity with the body and interacts with the physical and social environment. The body and the mind form one organism and interact through chemical and neural paths.

> There is quite a strong intertwining between corporeal regulation, survival and the mind; this takes place in the biological tissues and makes use of electric and chemical signals — all of this within Descartes' "res extensa" (the physical reign in which he includes the body and the surrounding environment, while he excludes the non-physical soul, assigned to the "res cogitans"). It is interesting to note that this happens at maximum intensity in a site not far from the epiphysis, the pineal gland in which Descartes attempted to imprison the non-physical soul. [ibid.]

On a subjective level emotions put us on our guard against choices that are associated with negative sensations and they make us favour those choices which are associated with positive sensations. In particular, when faced with the need to make a decision or judgement in particularly complex contexts, putting one's trust in an emotive impression can prove much more efficient than evaluating all of the pros and cons, or trying to remember, in their entirety, analogous past experiences. Most of the time, in the decision-making process — especially when we are dealing with problems that have multiple individual and social implications — we use strategies based on the results of past experiences in which we recognize some analogy with the present situation. The traces (often subconscious) that such experiences have left behind in us recall emotions and positive or negative sentiments whose physiological equivalents are defined by Damasio as *somatic markers*. In other words, the memory of the past emotion "marks" and therefore influences the final decision [Bechara et al., 1997]. This mechanism, which can follow a conscious or subconscious path, precedes any cost-benefit analysis that would require the intervention of other cortical regions and more time to complete.

> The emotional signal ( . . . ) can produce alterations in working memory, attention, and reasoning so that the decision-making process is biased toward selecting the action most likely to lead to the best possible outcome, given prior experience. The individual may not ever be cognizant of this covert operation. In these conditions we intuit a decision and enact it, speedily and efficiently, without any knowledge of the intermediate steps. [Damasio, 2003, pp. 148–149]

Now while it is true that the somatic marker does not deliberate for us — for generally, in order to make a decision, other and more complex assessments are often necessary — it is likewise true that it allows us to face a large number of everyday situations in an optimal way. Damasio maintains, in fact, that it is possible to use

> a cost/benefit analysis and proper deductive competence, but only after the automated step drastically reduces the number of options. Somatic markers may not be sufficient for normal human decision-making since a subsequent process of reasoning and final selection will still take place in many though not all instances. [Damasio, 1994, p. 173]

A series of important experiments conducted by Damasio and his collaborators on patients with lesions to the ventro-medial prefrontal cortex and to the limbic system highlighted how decision-making processes in such subjects are long and complex, because the individual finds him/herself making choices between options that are emotionally equivalent. The effect can be a total paralysis of the decision-making process or a choice that is disadvantageous to the individual. The clinical cases reported by Damasio (from the historic case of Phineas Gage and the patient called Elliot to the experiments conducted together with his collaborators) seem to corroborate the hypothesis that the capability to "process" the emotional content of somatic reactions is a fundamental component of *decision-making* processes. One of the crucial aspects that emerged from these and other studies is precisely the alchemy between emotion and cognition, an alchemy that sees distinct, and yet intimately connected, cerebral systems interacting (the more "archaic" limbic system and the "newer" neo-cortex, for instance). The term *affect-logic* [Ciompi, 1994] or *emotional intelligence* [Goleman, 1996] makes evident not only the present interest in the study of emotional phenomena, but also the role that these phenomena have among the typical functions of cognition. The complementariness of the limbic system and the neo-cortex, of the amygdala and the prefrontal lobes, makes clear the fact that each one of these constitutes an essential component of mental life.

## Towards an affect-logic

At this point one must ask oneself: how can the theory of *bounded rationality* help us reformulate the representation of the mind and to understand its conduct in the world? Furthermore, is a model of rationality conceivable that includes other methods of reasoning, perhaps just as complex and sophisticated?

The current debate, which has now moved beyond the well-known evidence reported in the studies of Simon and of Kahneman and Tversky, is characterized by a plurality of positions argued in great detail. The propositions of Gigerenzer, which he has also expressed in his recent *Rationality for mortals* [2008], constitute the object of a vigorous debate. Scholars such as Chater [2003] and Oppenheimer [2003] disagree with his positions: the first doubts that a simple heuristic such as *take the best* can be more realistic than other models; the second shows himself to be sceptical of the possibility that a judgement can base itself exclusively on a simple *recognition heuristic.*

Let us reconsider the famous experiment carried out by Gigerenzer and his collaborators on German cities. It could certainly happen that some individuals may know which, between two cities, is the smaller. However, according to Oppenheimer, the *recognition heuristic*, as conceived of by Gigerenzer, foresees that people will always indicate the city that they recognize as the biggest, even if they know that that city is small (but not whether or not it is smaller than the other city with which they are not familiar). In a series of analogous experiments on the recognition of the dimensions of cities known and unknown, Oppenheimer obtained a piece of evidence which would limit the extensive theoretical reliance on the recognition heuristic. These experiments show that recognition does remain an important cue for the making of a decision, but that it is not the only one (as affirmed by Gigerenzer and Goldstein), hypothesizing that people use strategies that are a bit more complex than the heuristics which are based on a single cue. Gigerenzer and Goldstein in fact affirm that the recognition heuristic

> (...) is a noncompensatory strategy: If one object is recognized and the other is not, then the inference is determined; no other information about the recognized object is searched for and, therefore, no other information can reverse the choice determined by recognition. [2002, p. 82]

In presenting the recognition heuristic Goldstein and Gigerenzer had pointed out that it does not always apply itself, nor does it always lead to correct inferences. For example, it does not apply itself when subjects know a considerable amount about the subject, but only in cases of limited knowledge, that is to say when not all of the objects are recognized. The authors maintain that even if a recognized object has a low value with respect to a pre-selected criterion (for example the dimensions of a city), it will still be chosen and preferred to the other object, which is not recognized. For example, if one were to ask an American to choose between two cities like Pisa and Prato, he/she would probably maintain, out of the simple fact of having recognized it, that Pisa is bigger, even if the individual knows that Pisa is not a very big city.

Naturally, these studies must face the problem of distinguishing mere recognition from other information that could be correlated with the choice to be made. This difficulty becomes more acute when one passes to the analysis of real-life situations as opposed to laboratory ones. The strength of simple recognition in the decision making process appears however to be sufficiently proved. If anything, the doubt is that this heuristic acts on its own. The very idea of a "toolbox" suggests the presence of countless strategies to be used according to the case at hand. Be that as it may, one aspect of Gigerenzer's proposal seems to be extremely convincing: whether the basic heuristics are only the simple and frugal ones, or whether other, more complex and elaborate heuristics go alongside them, an *ecological rationality* does not express itself through logical-formal rules and does not search for coherency, but rather only adaptive success. From this point of view the research in *The Adaptive Decision Maker* by Payne and his collaborators [Payne, 1993] appears to be quite realistic. In this book the authors affirm that the decision maker can choose in a strategic manner from among a certain *range* of decision-making methods, many of which are fast and frugal heuristics.

The "toolbox" metaphor contains in itself the idea of a decision maker being able to use many tools of different types and applications — some more simple, others more complex — in an opportune way, combining them, changing them when necessary and, finally, trying and re-trying them until the desired result is achieved. In the end, the more simple approaches and the more complex approaches prove to be essentially equivalent and in line with a very practical and effective attitude on the part of human beings (and other animals) towards the world that surrounds them.

CHAPTER

# 3

# The Neurobiological Bases of Decision Making

In little over a half a century we have learned more things about the brain than we had in the previous five thousand years. Until the middle of the previous century, the idea that biological research could reveal the brain's most hidden secrets would not even have been considered. Today, the rapid development of the neurosciences fosters the hope that soon it will be possible not only to explain the causes of many neurological and psychiatric diseases but also to explain aspects that have been considered inaccessible and non-measurable until now, such as aesthetic preferences, free will, the heterogeneity of preferences and of choice criteria, the role of emotions in decision-making processes and more. The result of these pioneering studies is retracing the traditional scientific disciplines, creating new transdisciplinary research programs such as neuroethics, neuroaesthetics, neuroeconomics and others.

Neuroeconomics — one of the most recent disciplines in the domain of the neurosciences — is using many of the results emerging from neurobiology. One need only think, for example, of the dopaminergic paths of the *mesolimbic system* which project themselves towards the *nucleus accumbens* in order to complete the neural system of desire and pleasure; of the role of "mu" receptors to which endogenous and exogenous opioids, the proteins that mediate human pleasure, link themselves; or of the subjective experiences of happiness that can be investigated with fMRIs and other non-invasive and multi-parametric methods of brain study. Decisions depend heavily upon emotions and sentiments, and as John Dewey affirmed in the past on a philosophical level, and Oatley and Johnson-Laird on a psychological one, emotions are born of a *difference in expectations* or of the *blockage of expectations* in connection with a certain event. And if the event is only a causal chain, the self, thanks to *consciousness*, can rise to the role of *agent*. Further, specific emotions depend upon the *meaning assessment* of the specific situation. As Tversky and Kahneman [1981] maintained, *earnings* or *losses* are associated with a purpose and, therefore, with intentionality. They represent, in fact, the contextual task that the decision maker must face, and therefore the internal representations of the decision maker's task configure the space of the decisional problem. In Paul Maclean's famous tripartite model of the brain, the evolutionary "conquest" in the passage from the reptile brain to the neocortex is that of an ever-greater flexibility. If the challenge in life is twofold and is to survive and to achieve reproductive success, and the two fundamental properties of living beings are their relative autonomy from events of the surrounding world and by their tendency to evolve, then the selective pressure which pushes towards complexity is precisely the need for an ever greater flexibility, adaptability and disposition towards change.

The presence of the neocortex seems to be indispensable in allowing an organism to drive away fear when facing a situation that in the past had been associated with that reaction [Levy, Servan-Schreiber, 1998]. Patients with *ventromedial frontal lesions*, studied by Damasio, do not stop experiencing emotions or sentiments, but rather lose the capacity of using them as "alarm systems" in representations of the future built on the basis of past lessons. According to Berthoz, the aim of memory is not to make us remember the past, but rather to allow us to predict the future. It also works "off-line". As we will see, the *somatic marker* emotionally marks our intentionality on the basis of experience and motivations. When the decision maker's internal representation does not have an immediate sensory content, but it is instead an abstract conceptualization, the emotional *bias* does not lose its importance, but it is no longer everything. In fact, while sensory *inputs* adhere to the objects of perception and change with them, the interpretations are relatively independent and decision making can take place on scales of time that are different from those of the reptile or protomammal brain, which are immediate and urgent.

Today many scholars believe that the interaction of economics, psychology and the neurosciences will soon cause a new model to emerge, a model able to synthesize all of those forms of knowledge which have thus far been neglected because they were considered to be immeasurable. It is of great importance that *brain imaging* methods have shown that decision-making processes principally activate a wide region between the *frontal lobe* and the *limbic system* which runs along the *corpus callosum* on the medial surface of the hemispheres, extending itself below the corpus callosum. In the same way, on a clinical level it is important that lesions to the *frontal lobe* have repercussions not only on the ability to make decisions that are advantageous to oneself and to others, but also on the ability to make socially appropriate decisions. As mentioned previously, neurological damage of this type deprives the victim of many of the abilities associated with intelligence, knowledge, logical ability, and language completely non-influential. Patients, in fact, become incapable of making decisions with regard to work, financial operations or relationships with others. They lose, in addition, those complex cognitive functions that allow for the gathering of information on ways of behaving and of deciding in analogous situations. When we are confronted with a situation similar to others we have faced before, we must not only face the specific problems in front of us, but we must also retrieve those emotional responses that will help us in the making of a decision.

## Reason and emotion: the false opposition

In the majority of cases we make choices on the basis of dynamics that are not entirely conscious. Even if decisions based on apparently formal reasoning strategies are possible, these strategies are always evaluated on the basis of the memory of past events. In situations of uncertainty, the system of emotions — like heuristics — helps us make quick decisions. It is, in fact, much more "economical" to make use of certain emotional memories than to analyze every detail of complex situations. One of the most heated debates in recent years in the domain of the neurosciences regards exactly that ability of emotions to influence our rational decisions.

As we have noted, in contrast to what Descartes maintained, reason and emotion are not separate spheres: indeed, reason is guided by the emotional assessment of the consequences of an action [Damasio, 1994]. The accumulated evidence from over fifty years of research renders it very difficult to produce arguments in favour of the classic thesis of a dualism between mind and body. On the other hand, just as the activity of the mind does not coincide with pure reasoning, the activity of the body does not limit itself to the exclusive satisfaction of physical needs. Along its evolutionary path the mind developed in order to improve the physical and psychological *performances* of human beings and to do so, it inevitably had to acquire information from the nervous structures that process the affective responses to stimuli and to memories. In this sense, the fact that an abstract model of rational decision making is inadequate in situations in which it is necessary to rapidly make a choice between different behaviours is also demonstrated by the fact that we are not always in a position to choose between definite options. As stated previously, in order to explain such dynamics, Damasio introduced the hypothesis of the *somatic marker* (a physiological indication able to discriminate between different behaviours), according to which emotions play a crucial role in determining an individual's rational behaviour, promoting behavioural responses to the environment that favour the individual's survival. Recalling William James's *central theory of emotions* [1890], Damasio hypothesizes that the physiological changes that appear in an organism in response to an emotional experience, and that represent deviations from the homeostatic equilibrium guaranteed by the structures of the limbic system, retroact on some neuronal circuits, thereby influencing the course of our assessments and, in part, directing our decisions [Damasio, 1994].

But what is the role of the *somatic marker*? It directs our attention to the negative results of an action, like an alarm signal that says: watch out for the danger that awaits you if you choose the option that leads to that result! The signal warns us about the negative results of the action, and thus leads us to choose among the alternatives that exclude it. It protects us from future losses and allows us to choose among fewer alternatives. It is obvious, however, that in normal decisions somatic markers can be insufficient, as in many cases there will be further reasoning and final choices. In summary, somatic markers are particular emotions and sentiments that have been connected, through learning, to the anticipated results of certain scenarios. When a negative somatic marker is associated with a particular future outcome, the combination functions as an alarm bell; when the marker is positive, it operates as an incentive [Damasio, 1994].

The somatic marker is an efficient interpretive tool for understanding the behaviour of patients with lesions to the *orbitofrontal cortex*. When this area is damaged, the representations of past experiences necessary to the production of a decision still enter into the working memory, but without their emotional content. Patients of this type are able to reflect upon problems, but without any emotional involvement. For example, the death of a person dear to the patient is completely devoid of the painful sensations which usually accompany such a loss. The orbitofrontal lesions cancel out the emotional processing of affective memories, modifying the *skin conductance response* (S.C.R.) mediated by the autonomous nervous system. In fact, patients with lesions to the pre-frontal cortex simply do not register these physiological indications: the patients appear incapable of generating skin conductance responses to memories. Therefore, situations that should alarm the patient leave him/her completely indifferent, and as a result they make inappropriate choices. This attests to the existence of a directly proportional correlation between the emotive flattening of these patients and their emotional physiological indications.

We must therefore ask: do physiological-emotional responses really mediate decision-making processes? Here as well researchers have attempted to provide an answer through tests such as the by now famous *risk-taking* test. This test is a game in which subjects choose cards from two decks; each card indicates a "play" monetary reward or penalty, and the goal is to earn as much money as possible. The two decks are different and the subjects learn by trial and error which of the two decks makes the player earn more play money. The cards of one deck cause the player to win high sums (100 dollars), but can also impose grave penalties (up to 1250 dollars);

in the other deck the rewards and penalties are more moderate (the subject can win 50 dollars and lose up to 100 dollars). While the control subjects gradually choose the latter deck, patients with orbitofrontal lesions prefer the deck that entails greater risk, perhaps because they are attracted by the frequent wins of 100 dollars, despite the fact that these wins end up being balanced by very high penalties.

The most interesting aspect of the experiment is the difference in the S.C.R. responses of the two groups. The subjects of both groups show a transitory increase in the S.C.R. when turning over a card, supported by a response of the autonomous nervous system to the reward or penalty. With time, however, in the control subjects these changes begin earlier. When these subjects are getting ready to choose a card from the riskiest deck, their S.C.R. rises considerably; when patients with orbitofrontal lesions are in the same situation, their S.C.R. of does not show any change. Therefore, the physiological evidence of a decision-making process mediated by emotion is missing [Bechara, Damasio and Damasio, 2000].

## Beyond the neurosciences and economics: ethological research

Despite the abundant evidence accumulated by researchers on this subject, the nature of the relationship between the frontal and limbic has still not been adequately explained. In situations that generate an *aversion to ambiguity* — namely situations, which most people avoid, in which we do not know the risks of a certain decision — brain imaging shows the activation of a part of the limbic area and of the frontal cortex, almost testifying to a "dialogue" between the two zones. In the interpretation of these events there are those who attribute the *aversion to ambiguity* to fear, and those who instead attribute it to a cognitive process of information processing based on a lesser availability of information. These different positions entail differences in the predictability of the behaviours. In fact, if the reaction of the brain to ambiguity were chiefly emotional, it would be rather difficult to learn to face it; if on the other hand it were chiefly cognitive, then one could slowly get used to ambiguity. In any case, the fMRI images do not help us to draw the necessary conclusions on such complex behaviours.

Researchers have not limited themselves to the inference of data and behavioural patterns from images of the brain in action, but they have also started to consider possible neuroendocrine mechanisms: in particular, those of oxytocin, a hormone secreted from the neuro-hypophysis during sexual relations, breast-feeding and in other activities that imply a relationship of trust, a factor which, as everyone knows, is decisive in economic interactions, from the purchasing of a house to investment in a pension fund.

Spinger and Fehr [2005] had some volunteers inhale oxytocin and observed that these subjects showed a greater willingness to entrust others with their money. Naturally, one must interpret these experiments with caution. The response in artificial conditions and during limited cognitive tasks can be very different from that in situations of everyday life.

Ethological contributions of great interest are joining the studies cited above. The use of animal subjects — monkeys in particular — can help us to understand the deep dynamics of our choices. The evidence reported by Harvard scholars Xiao, Padoa-Schioppa and Bizzi [2005] has shown the activation of neuronal areas correlated with the value that primates attribute to different objects. The objects in play were grapes and apples. It was observed, for example, that in the brain of a monkey who was called upon by researchers to choose between two drinks (apple juice and grape juice), two different groups of neurons of the *orbitofrontal cortex* were activated. It is plausible that these two groups of activated neurons correspond to the values that the monkey assigns to apple juice and to grape juice: in order to decide between the two drinks, the monkey would compare the values represented by these two populations of neurons. There are, however, other neurons that represent the final value chosen by the monkey, regardless of the juice. In these, if the value of the apple juice for the monkey is half of that of the grape juice, the act of taking the apple juice cuts the neuronal activity in half [Xiao, Padoa-Schioppa and Bizzi, 2005].

The question naturally arises: how can one infer the value attributed by the monkeys to the objects? And, above all, what is this value? The answers to these questions may be found in previous studies conducted on primates. In one of these studies in particular, if a grape and a piece of apple were offered to a monkey, the monkey would choose the grape. But if a grape and three or four pieces of apple were offered to the monkey, the monkey would choose without hesitation the pieces of apple, thus preferring quantity over quality [Padoa Schioppa et al., 2004]. Extending the model that emerges from these data to human beings, one could infer, with due caution, that the levels registered in the areas of the brain and the neuronal mechanisms involved in economic choices do not correspond to the conventional criteria of rationality. Obviously, questions about the psychological aspects and about the neural infrastructure that supports these choices remain unanswered, even if many indications suggest a strong involvement of the *orbitofrontal area*.

## Logical levels and explanatory gaps

Despite the considerable quantity of data and quantitative measurements regarding decision-making processes that have been provided by the non-invasive study of the living and dynamically active brain, many method-ological and epistemological problems remain. For example, the fMRI — especially with the *BOLD* (Blood Oxygenation Level Dependent) *effect* — only yields data on the flow, the haematic volume and its rapidity of transit in a certain cerebral region. Specifically, these techniques permit the study of cortical perfusion, which has been shown to increase in the course of neural activity: an increase limited to well-defined areas, the temporal reso-lution of which (in the order of seconds) reflects hemodynamic responses of the microcirculation correlated with neural activation. But neural activities are not directly observable with these techniques, and this is true even when leaving aside the cognitive limit of an unspecific "cortical activation", the meaning of which, whether excitatory or inhibitory, is not even known [Kennedy, Nowinski, Thirunavuukarasuu, 2003].

As far as EEG and MEG, these indicate the effect on the *cutaneous* surface of a variable electromagnetic field induced by the synchronous activity of neuronal *populations*. In order to be "valid", an EEG trace must come from the sum of the coordinated and concurrent activity of many neurons, neurons whose dendrites have been stimulated at the same time or that "discharge" in synchrony. Elevated levels of unsynchronized activity (as happens when the cortex actively analyzes a sensory stimulus or begins complex internal processes) do not produce the vector sum that is at all representative of all of the neural activity: the different electrical signals tend to cancel each other out, and are indistinguishable from other non-pertinent signals. Therefore, we have to infer a characterization of activity, of dynamics and of cerebral topology (the way in which the areas are connected amongst themselves) based upon indirect indications [Recchia Luciani, 2008].

These simple arguments — and others that could be adduced — suggest that the current methods of live brain imaging face severe limitations. When one studies the electrical activity of the brain (EEG or MEG), the limitations implied by the site (deep cerebral areas require invasive approaches) are added to the limitations of spatial resolution. If one studies metabolic or microcirculatory activity (PET or fMRI), the phenomena observed are intrin-sically "out of temporal scale" if the tests are not made for repeated and intense stimuli. It must be said that through "high resolution" EEG record-ings — made with thin networks of electrodes on the cortex of patients who are about to have surgical treatment for epilepsy — electrophysiology has discovered that small cerebral areas activated at a very high frequency (*high-gamma*) communicate with distant cerebral regions, not by the means of variations in activity over time (the well-known neural "firing"), or on the basis of frequency (the famous "40-Hz oscillations" between the thalamus and primary sensory cortices), but rather by virtue of the modulation and synchronization of phases on lower bands of frequency (theta) [Canolty et al., 2006]. Only recently have we understood that neurons "talk" among themselves in different ways, and that neurons do not exchange among themselves only "targeted" excitatory or inhibitory messages, but they also modify the neural electrochemical microenvironment through the secretion of paracrine which functions according to a hormonal model rather than according to the classic electrochemical model of the CNS. More generally speaking, if in a *functional segregation model* we identify more neural groups (more cerebral modules) whose function we have determined to be indispensable, in a *neural connectivity model* (anatomical, functional and real), the cerebral modules cooperate in order to make new functional properties emerge.

Regardless of these methodological restrictions, the epistemological problems prove to be consistent. The classical physical and chemical systems are closed, but the biological ones are open and irreducible to an algorithmic system (from equal *inputs* they do not give equal *outputs*). In systems of greater complexity, in which the result is determined by many variables, the prediction of the system's behaviour can be made only by statistical means, and this renders these systems *probabilistic*; that is, with changes of state that tend to be continuous rather than discrete. In these systems, the variations in measurable biological signals (collected with PET, fMRI, EEG, MEG, etc.) highlight the *systematic correlation* with events demonstrable on a psychological level: sometimes on a behavioural level, sometimes only on an introspective one. On this basis it is completely impossible to describe a causal relationship or a complex chain of causalities, even if the models and the paradigms that are at the basis of such a correlation are demonstrably valid and allow for predictions. It is for this reason that it is possible only to describe, but not to explain.

If one considers the issue of the overlapping of data and methodologies between economic models and psychological theories, it seems clear that it is exactly the centrality assigned to "measurability" which leads neuroeconomic researchers to take traditional economic models back into consideration, according to which all choices must be traced (at least ideally) to quantifiable factors such as prices and probabilities. A significant paradox follows from this, for it appears that neuroeconomics is not at all in discontinuity with the main economic paradigms, but rather in proximity with them. In fact, if on the one hand neuroeconomics offers the empirical support that classical economics has always held to be inessential, on the other hand it reaffirms the value of those same economic models as a guide in the exploration of the functioning of the brain and of individual behaviour. Furthermore, some of the same objections have been made to neuroeconomics as are directed at psychology: namely, that its models are descriptive and not quantitative.

We may therefore ask: if economic theories can help the neurosciences fill the explanatory gap between cerebral activity and behaviour, and if the cognitive neurosciences represent the new methodological approach of experimental economics, in what sense can the discovery of specific *patterns* of cerebral activation guide the creation of new economic hypotheses? Even if the fundamental assumptions and the critical methodological points call back into question the real predictivity of the proposed empirical models, neuroeconomists do not seem concerned about the meaning and utility of the experiments conducted in neuroeconomics; nor about the economic methodology and cognitive models that are at its foundation and how these are integrated into neuroscientific research; nor about the interpretation criteria of imaging data obtained from this type of experiment. All of this is of great significance for an integration of the spheres of the *homo economicus* and the *homo neurobiologicus*, an integration directed at an authentic representation of the real agent.

## A cognitive economy

It is the studies that derive from the work of Herbert Simon that set us on the path of a reasonable solution to these problems. His research into "cognitive economy" begins with psychologically-founded hypotheses on human behaviour and allows for the analysis of contexts excluded from standard analyses as they are intractable from a mathematical point of view. Distinct from macroeconomic rationalism, this line of research represents a strong indicator of future directions not only for experimental neuroeconomics, but also for an epistemology of economic psychology and a pioneering neuroethics.

Through the concepts of heuristics and *biases*, the "psychology of decision making" has clarified how the strategies, models and "cognitive shortcuts" that people use in making decisions are exposed (particularly when the decisions are made quickly or in situations of risk) to frequent errors which lead to the hypothesis of a sort of "regularity of error". On the other hand, sensory perception is always extremely complex and is characterized by stratagems and errors analogous to those of higher integrative activities. In the realm of decision making, the semi-conscious adoption of a heuristic allows for quick decision making and action without turning to complex analyses and measurements. Such heuristics are of use in many situations of ordinary life and are frequently founded on multiple experiences. However, although functional and necessary — because they allow for the saving of cognitive energies and time — these heuristics often push the mind into certain perceptive-evaluative misconceptions or *biases* that can become systematic and have serious effects in the decision-making sphere.

The *availability heuristic* makes us consider the probability or likely frequency of an event as being in proportion to the facility with which we recall meaningful circumstances or associations [Kahneman and Tversky, 1973]. Such circumstances and associations connected with frequent or more probable events are usually easier to memorize, more "available" in the memory, than those connected with events that are less frequent or probable. One can understand how such heuristics confer the advantage of a quick simplification of assessments and predictions that are otherwise very complex. But it is exactly this extreme simplification that can entail systematic errors. Be that as it may, beyond frequency and probability, the availability of an event is conditioned by various causes such as familiarity, emotional prominence and proximity in time. If these conditions are satisfied, the cognitive availability is very high, even when the objective frequencies and probabilities of the event are low. Using such a procedure, therefore, can mean on the one hand overestimating the frequency or probability of events coming to pass that are infrequent but have an emotional impact; on the other hand, it can mean underestimating the frequency or probability of events that are more usual but less sensational and available. Often in both economic choices and in everyday decisions one adopts the *anchoring and adjustment heuristic* [Tversky and Kahneman, 1981]: namely, that type of schema that directs our calculations on the basis of a tacit initial reference defined as an "anchor". If someone must express him/herself on the capability, sensitivity or intelligence of another person, he/she will adopt as a reference his/her own qualities in these same categories. Consequently, the level of the person to be judged will be over- or underestimated. Heuristics of this sort are used frequently in the daily economy: for example, when shopping in a supermarket we choose among many similar products the one whose brand is already known, judging it to be the best.

Considerable conditioning of the evaluative-decisional process is also carried out by the *framing effect* [Tversky and Kahneman, 1981], that is by the context of the choice and by the way in which the decision-making problems are presented. Thus the decision-making process may be divided into a *framing* phase and an *evaluation* phase. In the first phase the agent preliminarily examines the decision-making problem and *frames* the available options, their possible outcomes and the probabilities of such outcomes in relation to the choices to be made. Such *framing* is determined by the way in which the decision-making problem is set forth, and by the rules and habits of the decision maker. The essential aim of *framing* is to review and organize the options in order to simplify the following assessment, which is the real decisional choice. Research clearly shows the influence of *framing* on the evaluative and decisional procedures of individuals, because frequently the same questions or assertions set out with different or inverse expressions generate antithetic responses or reactions. How can we not think, in this instance, of the common expression about the glass being half full or half empty?

## The constraints and the possibilities

The first experimental results of neuroeconomics reveal new aspects of the complexity of the decision maker's nature, calling back into question one of the classic postulates of economic science: the egoistic *self-interest* of the *homo economicus*. More generally, the discovery of the role of psychology in economics is contributing to the demolition of the claims of a normative rationality in both microeconomic and macroeconomic choices. Naturally in experimentation and in theory the results, methods and approach of neuroeconomics can confirm or oppose the hegemony of economic science over psychology and the social sciences. This depends upon the paths that are followed with regard to epistemological orientation, methods, and the accuracy of experimental studies. For example, must individual material *self-interest* be considered as a variable independent from classic economics, or as an element of risk in the competitive economy? It is tempting to affirm that this material self-interest is incompatible with the new interactions and experimentations of psychology and economics, in particular with the concept of *methodological individualism* which sets individual reality as the focus of all economic research. Conversely, a rejection of the reality or importance of material *self-interest* would lead to a reaffirmation of holistic social interaction, in which the fundamental role of individuals, consumers and entrepreneurs is denied.

Luckily, interactions between disciplines are producing more and more valuable results. For example, Singer and Fehr [2005] maintain that economic theory has dealt only marginally with the connections between *beliefs* and *preferences*: connections which in fact are deep and could be studied by neuroeconomics in the interest of clarifying the complex relationships between the minds of economic agents during an interaction. Moreover, understanding these dynamics is fundamental to the recognition of the real micro-determinant factors of choices and to the foundation, therefore, of a new typology of economic analysis. The skill of "mind reading," so to speak, will obtain considerable benefits from a positive interaction between game theory and the *theory of mind*. Such an interaction is intimately connected with the classic problem of mind-body relations, and therefore to the relationship between mental and physical events: a problem which has been subject to extended debate by researchers in the philosophy of mind and in disciplines such as psychology, biology, physiology, and more recently the cognitive neurosciences.

An important element of neuroeconomics is the use of probability calculation in order to deal with decisions in situations of uncertainty. According to the objectives that individuals or groups set and the decisions that they make it is possible to derive their neurobiological correlates using *brain imaging* methods. Naturally, in order to identify an objective with precision it is first necessary to assess the utility of each action, in order to then calculate the probability of that objective. As in any scientific field, it will be empirical evidence that legitimizes this emerging area of research.

Beyond the exclusively scientific dimension, neuroeconomic research pushes us to look at concepts such as free will, predictability and decision-making dynamics very differently. Neuroeconomics provides a very different perspective on free will and on the predictability and determinism of our decisions. In a time marked by uncertainty, the free will of human beings becomes an issue that is as problematic as it is crucial. New questions and new explorations are already arising, encouraging the creation of transdisciplinary spaces well beyond the interactions of neuroeconomics and of neuroethics.

## Naturalizing decision making

The many experiments and studies on the neurobiological bases of decision making through *brain imaging* technologies have created a formidable challenge to the attempts to provide a unitary account of economic choices [Piattelli Palmarini, 2005]. This is in fact demonstrated by the birth of *neuroeconomics* [Camerer, Loewenstein and Prelec, 2004; Glimcher, 2003; Zak, 2004], which has become a meeting point of neuroscientific, economic and psychological studies that offer the possibility of mediating between the abstract models of neoclassical economics and actual human behaviour. In short, neuroeconomics represents the domain par excellence "where psychology and economics meet" [Chorvat, McCabe and Smith, 2004].

Contrary to behaviorists, neuroeconomists attempt to reveal the *black box*, the mind of the agent, constructing biologically-rooted models that faithfully describe real cognitive and computational abilities, thus explaining an important part of individual behaviour [Camerer, Loewenstein and Prelec, 2004]. The first experimental results of neuroeconomics reveal new aspects of the complexity of decision-making behaviour, disproving one of the classic postulates of economic science: the egoistic *self-interest* of the *homo economicus*. In that sense, neuroeconomics is offering new and promising critical elements to *game theory*. For example, the *ultimatum game*, one of the most famous games ever invented by modern experimental economics — a game that takes the theory of the *Nash equilibrium* to a higher level — demonstrates that in order to predict the behaviour of players it is necessary to consider a utility function that, distinct from the "classic" theory of games based on *pay-offs* (the maximization of one's own utility/earnings), takes into consideration the *trade-offs* between one's own consumption and a sense of justice, of *fairness*. If discussing justice, fairness, and moral values on the one hand enriches neuroeconomics with contributions that go beyond the sum of the evidence produced by the neurosciences or by the economic sciences, on the other hand it prompts epistemological and ethical openings that have strong repercussions in the debate on consciousness and free will [Loasby, 1976].

Up until a few years ago it would have been unthinkable to try to understand what happens in our brain while we are making a decision that has moral implications, or to determine whether or not a neural substrate of the representation of values exists. Today, instead — thanks to the development and progress achieved by new methods — such queries have not only become part of the legitimate objectives of scientific research, but have also received the first responses which put deep-rooted philosophical convictions to the test. This is demonstrated by numerous experiments thanks to which researchers — observing the activation of cerebral areas in volunteers submitted to various moral dilemmas — have started to understand that there is a neural substrate involved in moral judgements. William Safire [2003] was the first to use the term "neuroethics" in the sense of "bioethics of the brain". The neuroscientist Michel Gazzaniga has expanded the horizons of the term, affirming that

( . . . ) neuroethics is more than just bioethics for the brain. As the field develops, we need to expand its scope and its mission. Much of the discussion in neuroethics so far has, once again, been among non-scientists. It is time for neuroscientists to jump into the fray. I would define neuroethics as the examination of how we want to deal with the social issues of disease, normality, mortality, lifestyle, and the philosophy of living *informed by our understanding of underlying brain mechanisms*. It is not a discipline that seeks resources for medical cure, but one that places personal responsibility in the broadest social and biological context. It is — or should be — an effort to come up with a brain-based philosophy of life. [Gazzaniga, 2005, p. xv]

In conclusion, although new discoveries in neuroeconomics and neuroethics are coming one after the other very quickly, it is necessary to refrain from feelings of naive enthusiasm. Researchers of the previous century succeeded in explaining material, in dominating energy, in inventing information technology, but forgot about the sensitive body and separated reason and emotion, thus reducing the decision-making process to abstract axioms unaffected by time. Certainly, studies on decision-making processes are slowly recovering the subtlety of intentionality, of emotivity, of subjectivity, and overcoming the rigid barriers of economic *rational choice*, but at this stage to be optimistic would be both unhelpful and premature. Despite the tumultuous growth of neuroscientific data, we are still quite far from mastering the complexity of choice processes.

# CHAPTER

# 4

# Towards a Science of Free Will?

Two things fill the mind with ever new and increasing admiration and awe, the oftener and the more steadily we reflect on them: the starry heavens above and the moral law within. I have not to search for them and conjecture them as though they were veiled in darkness or were in the transcendent region beyond my horizon; I see them before me and connect them directly with the consciousness of my existence.

— IMMANUEL KANT

How the idea of ethics has changed since the times of the philosopher from Königsberg! An enormous quantity of investigation — neurobiological and anthropological, philosophical and psychological research, but also trans-cultural, gender, age, race and religious studies — have revealed the extreme complexity of ethics, the effect of our long evolutionary history. Studies that are ever more acute and perceptive are gradually revealing the patterns of activities underlying judgements and moral choices. These developments have added difficult new questions to the age-old (and still unanswered) questions of philosophy. For example: if the rules of ethics are inscribed in the brain, what is left of free will? Can we still call ourselves free or is freedom only an illusion? Are there neurobiological structures on which to build a system of ethics valid for all human beings? And if there are, what concept of freedom is at the foundation of that system?

Much of the experimental evidence on the role of emotions and reasoning in the moral sphere [Hauser, 1996] shows that the inquiry into moral judgement has considerable affinities with the research carried out by linguists on how human beings use language well before knowing grammar. It was in this way that the hypothesis was advanced that the human species may be equipped with an innate sense of what is right and what is wrong — a sort of *universal moral grammar* at the basis of our judgements — analogous to the Chomskyan *universal linguistic grammar* [Chomsky, 1957]. A group of Harvard researchers guided by Mark Hauser tried to verify this hypothesis by using experimental material chiefly composed of clinical evidence, evolutionary data, developmental psychology data and neuropsychological tests [Hauser, 2006]. These studies — which in fact have moved the focus from the role of emotions in moral intuition to the grammar of action (namely to the invariance and regularities of actions) — have explained how people develop moral judgements on the basis of subconscious principles, well before they show emotional reactions. In other words, just as one asks in what way language is different from acoustic signals, one can also ask what differentiates a moral dilemma from a practical one. According to this account, moral judgements originate from a "subconscious" analysis of the causes and the effects of an action, after which emotion (for example, a sense of guilt) follows. If this were the case, human beings would be *instinctual jurists* in a certain sense, that is, agents equipped with a mental device that provides them with a grammar of action corresponding to an instinctive sense of what is right and what is wrong [Hauser and Spelke, 2004]. This implies a clear distinction between the grammar of moral judgement (inaccessible to consciousness), and action guided by emotion and *ex-post* rational justifications. This distinction is demonstrated by patients with functional problems or brain lesions, who, although their knowledge of moral rules is intact, behave in an abnormal way as they have lost the ability to feel appropriate emotions.

These studies on human ethics have naturally lead to the analysis of the whole system of ethical thought, in which emotions, although important, are not dominant. The study of emotions shows, in fact, that ethics are intertwined with the processes that govern life and the functioning of the body, and that it is exactly from this intertwining that there arise the contradictions of the good or bad reasons that each person invokes in order to justify his/her behaviour to oneself and to others. The emergence of these contradictions is perhaps one of the most interesting results of experimental research, and the fact that jurists have neglected this research has unfortunately placed a limit on their investigations. A more profound knowledge of these studies would considerably enrich the legal vocabulary, and would also indirectly equip us with useful criteria for facing issues tied to scientific progress.

The idea of a moral faculty acquired over the course of evolution and corresponding to specific cerebral structures can suggest more general reflections. We may imagine that a primary moral competency could be the foundation of a disposition towards tolerance, equality and comprehension between human beings, reaching beyond different ethnicities, religions and cultures.

# Does free will exist?

In the 1970s the neuroscientist Benjamin Libet set up a famous experiment on the timing of "conscious awareness". He observed that voluntary actions are preceded in the brain by specific electrical alterations which occur 550 thousandths of a second before the beginning of an action. More precisely, people subjected to an experiment become conscious of the intention to carry out an action 350–400 thousandths of a second after the specific electrical change that indicates the readiness to carry out the action has occurred in the brain, and 200 thousandths of a second before the action itself [Libet, 1996]. The voluntary decision is made, therefore, without a contribution from consciousness. It is consciousness, however, that decides the outcome of the action, through facilitations or inhibitions. This means that, within certain constraints, free will does have a specific role of its own. Consciousness would not be the starting point of the voluntary action, but would instead "decide" whether or not to carry out that action.

If we consider the temporal sequence of inception and control of voluntary actions, we conclude that this sequence is the result of collaboration between multiple motor areas internal and external to the cerebral cortex. The cerebral areas involved in the planning and execution of an action, however, are not able on their own to activate the planned movement: they must collaborate with the *basal ganglia*, sub-cortical structures close to the *limbic system* which do not fall under the control of consciousness. In any case, at the origin of intention and of the realization of an action there is emotional memory, which is not directly controlled by conscious awareness [Koch, 2007]. Between the beginning of an action and its realization a lot of time can even elapse: the time of *conscious awareness* which implies the activation of the frontal cortex. In the realization of a voluntary movement the role of cerebral areas that are not consciously controlled is decisive.

But, if that is how things are, can we still say that we possess of free will, or is it just an illusion? And what conception of freedom is there at the foundation of moral judgement? Certainly, we would be far from Kantian freedom. In fact, a subject evaluates and decides using all of the areas of the brain that over the course of evolution have been selected for the control of actions. Furthermore, he/she uses information originating from cerebral areas that represent the neural basis of the subjective experiences of emotions and desires. Moreover, the fact that in this activity other faculties collaborate with consciousness (although beyond its control) is not a discovery of contemporary neurobiology: Freud had already spoken of this. With the activation of cortical areas — an activity experienced subjectively as the ability to judge — the agent reflects upon the options that he/she has [Berthoz, 2004]. The agent's decision whether or not to undertake a certain action is influenced by whether the cerebral areas in which emotional memory is deposited, memory accumulated over the course of the agent's individual experience, send him/her positive or negative signals (which Edelman defined as *values* and Damasio as *somatic markers*). In a subject without serious psychopathological disorders, both the rational evaluation and the emotional one are experienced as personal capacities, even if some are accessible to the control of consciousness and others only indirectly. However, we experience our individual identity not only because we think autonomously, but also because we have a subconscious "ability to feel", typical of human beings, developed over the course of our life experience (subconscious awareness).

In the Western philosophical tradition there are theories of free voluntary action that are very different from the concept of a solipsistic freedom of the rational subject that is indifferent to the body and its prerogatives. These theories not only provide a good model for how we have experiences in the "first person" or the way in which we exercise freedom, but also for the way in which neurophysiologists describe voluntary action. How can we not recall, in this connection, Aristotle's debate with Plato that saw the Stagirite affirm that each practical choice comes from a *deliberate desire*, that is, from the interweaving of reasoning and desire?

> What affirmation and negation are in thinking, pursuit and avoidance are in desire; so that since moral virtue is a state of character concerned with choice, and choice is deliberate desire, therefore both the reasoning must be true and the desire right, if the choice is to be good, and the latter must pursue just what the former asserts. [Aristotle, 1973: p. 463]

Aristotle had sensed that, in decision making, thought and desire move together in a coordinated manner, and that it is in this coordination that the specific ability of an individual to realize him/herself has its origin. Naturally, along with the regulating activity of consciousness other spheres collaborate — sensation, perception, memory, imagination, desire, emotion and sentiment — which, if adequately understood, reveal a human complexity that is for consciousness a necessary condition for making an effective choice.

## Value systems and hierarchies

It is plausible to believe that our adaptive behaviours are influenced by biologically-determined *value systems* that regulate our experiences. Each one of these value systems would be correlated, according to the circumstances, to a type of neurotransmitter: *dopamine*, present in the basal ganglia and in the encephalic trunk, which acts as a reinforcement system in learning; *serotonin*, which regulates mood and other biological functions such as sleep, hunger, etc.; and *acetylcholine* which modifies thresholds in the state of wakefulness, in sleep, and so on [Gazzaniga, 2005]. Our ontogenetic and phylogenetic history makes criteria of choice which have been "memorized" in emotions available to us, without which our lives would be qualitatively poor, and indeed, our very existence in danger.

It is emotions and heuristics, essential functions of natural logic, that provide us with indications on how we should act in certain circumstances, and that tell us, much more quickly than a reasoning process, what we have to be afraid of, what we can desire, and so on. If because of cerebral lesions we are unable to use these indications, our choices will be poor, even if our capacity to reason remains intact. Some studies conducted on the functioning of memory have allowed us to understand the ways in which our minds creatively use memorized experience in order to face new situations, making use of both the experience accumulated by the species, and of the experience accumulated by the individual [Oliverio, 2008]. It is exactly that *sensory memory* — in which personal experience, interpersonal experience and the history of our species are permanently connected — that makes up the material basis of our *personal identity*.

One must, however, ask: can emotions and heuristics — those complex individual characteristics that help us respond appropriately to the demands of the natural and social environment — form the basis of a set of ethics valid for all human beings? Such a thing would be rather improbable: human beings are much more than this. We have thought, language, culture: in brief, a second nature [Edelman, 2006] that we, precisely as natural beings, developed and that allows us to make free choices.

## The biological structures of inter-subjectivity

The discovery of *mirror neurons* has shown that there is a very close link between perception and movement [Gallese, 2008]. According to this evidence, perception is an ability to interpret an object in terms of possible movements and actions that the person who perceives it could carry out in relation to it. In and of itself, therefore, an object is a hypothesis or a plan of action. Experiments conducted by Rizzolatti and his group [Buccino et al., 2004] highlighted the activation of the same motor areas both in the case where the test subject was asked to carry out an action on an object exposed to perception, and in the case in which he/she was not asked to perform any action in relation to the object. Rizzolati called *mirror neurons* those neurons that are activated when we perceive an object as a hypothesis of action.

This study has further implications: the activation of mirror neurons allows us to understand the intentions of someone concentrated on carrying out an action. That is, they make us able to understand the intentions of others on the basis of our "intentional vocabulary", and it is in this way that we are able to interpret the emotions of others [Iacoboni, 2008]. Both clinical data and the data obtained through brain imaging or electro-stimulation show that, when we feel an emotion and when we perceive the emotion of another person from the expression on his/her face, the same cerebral areas are activated. This leads to the belief that the brain is not a mechanical apparatus, but a semantic-intentional system. What is more, perception does not passively reproduce images that are separate and distant from us, but rather it puts a complex set of knowledge at our disposal. In other terms, through perception we answer the question: how can I behave with respect to an object, given that my body is made in a certain way, that my body has certain abilities and limitations, and that, with respect to such an object, I feel a certain emotion? The capacity to experience, in the first person, the intentions of others and to share with them intentions and emotions allows us to perceive others as being similar to us, establishing the basis of inter-subjective relationships and relations of reciprocal recognition.

## Rationality versus emotions in moral judgement

In a study by Greene and other neuroscientists conducted with fMRI [2004] and directed at ascertaining the presence of a conflict between the areas of the brain involved in emotions (those that make us feel horrified at the idea of hurting someone) and those involved in rational analysis (that calculate how many lives are lost and saved), it was noted that when the individuals being questioned reflected on scenes in which they needed to kill someone with their own hands, different areas in their brains were activated. One area included the medial parts of the *frontal lobes*, an area involved in the emotions expressed in social interactions; another included the *dorsal lateral surface of the frontal lobes*, which is involved in mental calculations, including reasoning processes of a non-moral nature; and the third was the *anterior cingulate cortex*, a band that is ancient in an evolutionary sense and that is found at the base of the internal surface of the cerebral hemispheres, which registered a conflict between an impulse originating in one zone of the brain and a signal coming from another. When the individuals reflected on a situation that did not require them to put their hands on another person, the brain reacted differently: the only area to activate itself was the one associated with rational calculations [Marcus, 2002].

In this regard, the famous experiment called the "train dilemma" [Hauser, 2006] is still of great interest, as it has made an important contribution towards clarifying the role of the moral spheres in our decisions. In the experiment the subject was asked to imagine the following situation: during a morning walk the subject sees a train hurtling along some tracks. The conductor of the train has collapsed and is unconscious. Along the tracks there are five men at work, oblivious to the danger. Near to where the subject is standing there is a lever which, if pulled, would divert the train towards a service track, thus saving the lives of the five individuals. If the observer were to pull the lever, however, the train would inevitably hit one worker who is at work on the other track. Here we have the dramatic dilemma: should one pull the lever and kill one man in order to save five? Almost everyone would consider pulling the lever to be the right choice.

A different circumstance was also considered. From a bridge above the tracks the subject sees the runaway train. The only way to stop it is to throw down onto the tracks a person who is standing beside the observer. Should he/she do it? Both of the dilemmas make us face the choice of sacrificing one life in order to save five. According to utilitarian parameters — calculating that which would produce the greatest good for the greatest number of people — the dilemmas appear to be the same. And yet the majority of the people questioned responded that, while they would pull the lever in the first case, in the second case they would not throw the person onto the tracks, even though they could not explain their own choice.

Other studies have shown how neurological patients, who feel dulled emotions because of frontal lobe lesions, transform themselves into perfect utilitarian agents, maintaining that it is completely reasonable to throw someone from the bridge onto the tracks. This evidence led Hauser to invoke an analogy between moral sense and language [Hauser, Chomsky and Fitch, 2002]. According to this analogy, just as in Chomsky's model [Chomsky, 2000] everyone is born with a "universal grammar" that obligates us to analyze discourse in terms of its grammatical structure, we are equipped, from birth, with a universal moral grammar which leads us to analyze human actions in terms of their moral structure, in both cases with little awareness that we are doing so.

## At the roots of evolution

Psychological studies have shown that expressions such as the instinct to prevent pain, a sense of fairness, group loyalty, authority and purity — cardinal expressions of our moral sense — have deep evolutionary roots [Wilson, 1993]. The instinct to prevent pain, which provokes tremors in us at the thought of throwing a man over a bridge, is present in some primates, who, when presented with the possibility of pulling on a chain that would provide food for the primate but would also cause an electric shock to another monkey, do not pull the chain. Respect for authority is correlated to the hierarchies of dominance and pacification which are extremely wide-spread in the animal world. The sense of fairness recalls the behaviour called *reciprocal altruism*, in which the willingness to help another evolves as long as the favour helps the person receiving it more than it costs the person who performs it, and as long as the person who receives it is willing to return the favour when he/she has the opportunity to do so [Axelrod, 1984]. The sense of community — an attitude which pushes individuals towards sharing and sacrificing themselves for an impersonal goal — could derive from the empathy and the solidarity that we feel towards family members and non-family members of the same social group. In this sense, from an evolutionary point of view, and given shared interests, loving one's neighbour could derive ultimately from a motive of self-interest, and this would explain how moral sense can be, at the same time, both universal and variable.

## The inverted perspective: the reciprocity of ethics

What neurobiology teaches us about spheres of the mind like sensation, perception, memory, emotion, sentiment, intentionality and inter-subjectivity must be the object of careful reflection for an individual that is considering how to act from a moral point of view [Gazzaniga, 1997]. We must ask ourselves why, if the distinction between what is right and what is wrong depends on our cerebral structures, we should consider this distinction to be more real or important than the difference, for example, between black and white. In other words, how can we show that evils like the Holocaust and racial intolerance are wrong for everyone, and are not just repugnant to us? It is plausible to believe that we are born with a rudimental moral sense, and as soon as we develop reasoning to operate with it, reality obliges us to come to certain conclusions, and not others.

Two factors exist which direct any rational and social agent equipped with a spirit of self-preservation to act morally. One of these factors is the prevalence of games that are not "zero-sum" [Kreps, 1992]. Under many circumstances, if two individuals behave altruistically they generate situations that are objectively better than situations generated by egotistical behaviours. The inclination to altruistic behaviour, then, does not depend on the brain or on a supernatural power, but rather upon a natural evolutionary-adaptive improvement. The other factor is a characteristic of rationality itself, or at least the natural result of objective thought about social interaction. If I want to be taken seriously when I ask someone to do something that is important to me, I cannot do so while favouring my interests over the other person's. The essence of this idea — which could be defined as the *inter-changeability of perspectives* — is present in the most important moral philosophies of history [Rawls, 1971]. This is a moral value superior to our *particulare* — supported by evolution, but fed by rationality — that can push us to open up to an ever greater number of human beings. In this sense, morality is larger than our inherited moral sense and this fact has important consequences. Even when the motivations of our adversaries appear disconcerting, these motivations may derive not from psychiatric symptoms that lead to amoral behaviour, but instead from a set of imperative and universal ethics like our own. In a conflict, accepting that another could be guided by moral motivations that are not dishonest can be a first step towards the identification of a common ground [Rawls, 2004].

In light of these considerations, can we reasonably maintain the existence of a *universal moral sense*? Certainly, emotions help us to know and act, but how do we place them at the foundation of a set of universal ethics? There is no doubt that neurobiological knowledge enriches our reflection on this question. We know that our brain is formed to function in the environment to which it is exposed. We also know that the plasticity of our brain is such that it can be used to modify even our own identity. In spite of this, science will not relieve us of the responsibility of answering both age-old and new questions, and not even large amounts of evidence will lift us above the responsibility linked to our choices [Parfit, 1989]. Like the other senses, the moral sense is vulnerable to illusions: it often confuses morality with purity, it imposes taboos that put some ideas beyond question, and it has the awful propensity to always consider itself to be on the "right" side. In the worst case scenario, our foolish instinctual behaviour itself can be considered a virtue. Be that as it may, a science focusing on the moral sense does not call morality itself into question [Boella, 2008]. Indeed, it can help to improve that sense, allowing us to see beyond the illusions determined by the evolution of culture and to concentrate on objectives that we can share and defend. It is not naive to believe that human beings will become better when their true nature reveals itself to them.

CHAPTER

**5**

# The Altruistic Gene

It is probable that without the tendency towards competition, which is firmly rooted in human biology structure and was already clearly described by Heraclitus in the fifth century BC, civilizations would not even have existed. Starting with the research of Charles Darwin [1859], numerous studies have shown that competition is an essential factor in selection within the human species, and speaking in general terms, an essential factor in human evolution. For the great English naturalist, living beings represent the result of a tough selection process which rewarded the species capable of surviving in a particular environment. Over the course of the millennia, as the result of extraordinary selective pressure, human beings have structured their behaviour by means of connections (which have become more and more complex) between phylogenetic programs and pre-determined behavioural repertoires, between motivational states and psychological-moral spheres. The cerebral functions of human beings are themselves the result of a selection carried out over the course of phylogenesis and on the basis of anatomical-functional variations present at the birth of every single animal. In its embryonic stage, in fact, the brain is characterized by an overabundance of neurons and by dynamics that closely recall the process of natural selection proposed by Darwin as the basis for the evolution of living species: a process through which, based on the activity being performed, some groups of neurons die while others survive and become stronger [Edelman, 1987/1995].

If it is true that it is our genetic heritage that defines us, and that the first form of competition is of a biological nature, it is likewise true that it is the plasticity of the brain that allows human beings to have experiences, to construct versions of the present out of these experiences, to imagine the future, and to organize and plan the future according to their own needs. Therefore, competition is sustained not only by biological mechanisms, but also by various psychological dynamics: the need for self-affirmation, for success and for possession; the rivalry with a father figure in order to conquer the attentions of one's mother; the need to meet the expectations of a group; the need to obey authority figures; the analysis of the cost-benefit relationship, and many others. This group of factors, which prompt or limit competitive behaviour, make identifying competition with aggressiveness implausible.

When in the 1970s the sociobiological trend of evolutionism extended the Darwinian paradigm to human societies — maintaining that the system of nature is always competitive and that human beings are part of that pattern — many had the impression that the solution to one of the great problems of theoretical biology had been found. Richard Dawkins [1976] affirmed that organisms are only extensions of the gene, and that every individual acts with his/her best interests in mind. Therefore, even when an individual sacrifices him/herself for others, he/she contributes to the reproduction of his/her own genetic heritage. In this sense, altruism and behaviour directed at the improvement of the conditions of single individuals and of society are pure illusions.

Sociobiologists reject the idea that altruistic behaviour is useful to the species [Wilson, 1979]. On a selective level such behaviour could not take place, as the *discrete unit* of selection lies not in the population or single organism, but in the individual gene. They argue that if in an animal population there are mutations which determine changes in behaviour — for example, some animals sacrifice themselves for the community and others do not — something very simple will happen: the animals that sacrifice themselves will die out and those that do not will survive. The fact that the population benefits from the altruistic behaviour of one animal is therefore irrelevant, as the entity that selection influences is not the population, but rather the single individual.

One could object to this thesis by pointing out that it is not the genes that are acting, but the animals. For example, an animal that sacrifices itself for its offspring is indifferent to the fact that its own genes are advantaged by this action. Despite the fear of death, an animal that has reached a certain evolutionary level sacrifices itself just the same. In this sense, if it is plausible to maintain that there is no behaviour determined by the "principles of a species", it is conversely implausible to maintain that "only the egoism of genes exists". Of course, it is always the gene that replicates itself — and strictly speaking the animal does not sacrifice itself for its species but rather for its own genes. But behaviour is always the prerogative of the individual animal, even more because the gene is not at all identifiable with the individual organism. There is always something that transcends animal behaviour, and as a consequence, it is unjustified to see in animal behaviour only "egoistic dynamics".

Sociobiologists, therefore, place enormous importance on the role of the individual gene, but they do not consider the fact that it is the organism in its totality which allows the gene to survive. Further, we must not exclude the possibility that some genes which appear to be devoted to their own selective and competitive advantage have relations and connections with other genes which bring about evolutionary advantages through biological and chemical laws which are still unknown to us. Perhaps it is not far-fetched to affirm that a population derives reproductive advantages precisely from the altruistic behaviour which adaptively favours that population compared to another population that is not familiar with this behaviour. Contrary to the conclusions of Konrad Lorenz — according to whom animals demonstrate little intraspecific aggression — in the animal world altruistic behaviour is in fact present. But while in the animal world altruistic behaviour is limited to the examples which involve reciprocity, in the human world sacrifice for one's group is founded on the eminently ethical-rational universalization capacity of human beings. Therefore, one could not say that behind altruism there is only egoism, but rather that behind this egoism there is the need for the altruism of self-preservation [Gould, 2008].

Avoiding the risk of anthropomorphization one can affirm that while altruistic animal behaviour (which often reaches extreme sacrifice) generally arises in an effort to correspond with analogous intraspecific behaviour (tied to the ability to identify the animal that was altruistic in the past), the altruism of a human being can be directed both towards people who have been altruistic with him/her and towards others who are completely unknown. This is because altruism in human beings is marked by universal characteristics, linked as it is to traditions and values. This adaptive strategy — which modified the egoistic urges present in the initial phases of evolution and stabilized itself at the level of cultural evolution — then transformed itself into a true self-preservation mechanism.

Generally speaking, one could consider the evolution of animal behaviour — in the sequence from exclusive egoism to altruism towards one's relatives, to reciprocal altruism between animals that recognize each other individually, to the "universal" altruism of human beings — as a tendency to free oneself more and more from the mechanism of self-preservation, which is on the other hand essential to the survival of the species. Higher animals have always been in competition with animals similar to them for the conquest of territory and for means of sustenance. Nevertheless the principle according to which behaviour, and above all human behaviour, is founded only on the perpetuation of genes, and that organisms act solely on the basis of an egoistic tendency, is difficult to maintain. In reality, the central idea of sociobiology is supported by an obvious truth: the genes able to survive and multiply in the environment prevail over those that are not capable of doing so. Therefore, organisms whose behaviour is determined by these genes have a greater chance of surviving than others.

Now, if it is reasonable to maintain that human action is in large part governed by the evolutionary principle of the diffusion of genes, then to consider sympathy, friendship and altruism as pure illusions would mean maintaining that every organism is seeks only its own good at the expense of others, and this is completely unprovable.

## Domains and dynamics of competition

But what are the dynamics of competition between individuals and how do they work? It must be said, first of all, that competitive behaviour is present in every single situation and that the more intense the competition, the more significant its effects are. The competitors express diversities, asymmetries and dissonant profiles that are often incompatible both individually and collectively. It is therefore not surprising that the victory of one corresponds with the frustration of the other. Although the competitors' *being in a relationship* is an essential factor of competitive dynamics, actors are commonly different one from the other almost to the point of "disidentification", and the intensity of the competition depends on the degree of this differentiation, as well as on other factors.

In fact, each competition is defined by the importance of the stakes and by the characteristics of the participants: their strength and abilities, their charisma, their personalities and expression of their selves, and their perceptions of their allies and adversaries. If the individuals in a competition are not of equal strength, the imbalance renders the results predictable. On the other hand, a competition in which the actors attribute little importance to the objectives being pursued; in which the necessary asymmetries are played down; in which factors of interference, distraction, and emotional and affective disinvestment are present — a competition in which these factors are present will prove to be ineffective.

Generally speaking, competition expresses itself in a two-phased sequence: a period of progressive increase until a peak is reached, and then a reduction phase in which the competition decreases until disappearing completely. This trend — which manifests itself in sporting competition as well as in social and military conflicts — is characterized by two opposing psychological needs: the need to seek confrontation, to establish it and amplify it, and the need to reduce and neutralize the conflict. The natural tendency to radicalize competition and the opposing tendency to reduce it are constant factors in social and military conflicts.

In particular, sporting competition [Hewston, Stroebe and Stephenson, 1996] — which is a conflict with its own distinctive means and patterns — is regulated by rules designed to safeguard the adversaries. The competitors, in fact, must vie for only one thing, victory; every other expression is excluded. The prohibitions and the penalties specified in the written regu-

lations, laws, customs, legal procedures, and normative institutions have as
their objective the inhibition of violence through the institution of rules that
are valid *erga omnes*". Excess energies are in this way channelled along pre-
established axes and directed towards non-harmful goals. Outside of the
"field" defined by the rules, competition dies out and peace prevails.
Infraction of the rules and transgression of the limits entails reproof, sanc-
tions, and/or expulsion from the system.

Athletic competition — which takes place either in a neutral area or on
the home field of one of the competitors — requires forms of sharing and of
"co-presence". Generally, reciprocal respect and shared feelings among the
participants emphasize the dynamics of competition rather than minimizing
them. In some types of solitary races competition assumes — through
dynamics of imagination and interiorization of the adversary — fantastic
dimensions in the minds of the competitors. These fantastical images constitute an enormous reserve of symbolic material for the satisfaction of
psychological requirements that the actual competition may not have met
[Trevi, 1993]. This focusing on an imaginary and more intense version of the
competition facilitates learning and creativity, tools that are useful in the
improvement of the participants' results. Moreover, this imaginary work
increases the participants' capacities, enriching the emotional life of both
individuals and groups. There is a perfect symmetry between the satisfaction of the individual's various desires and motivations and the individual's
aesthetic experience of the competition. Competitive dynamics — which
flow from the mental representations, perceptions, emotions and actions of
the initial phases of the competition — satisfy the various motivational
spheres of the participants.

Between athletic competition and war there is not only an isomorphic
continuity, but also a tendency to alternation: where the first one takes place
the second one cannot be carried out, and vice versa. The Greeks, as is well
known, suspended hostilities every time athletic games of a certain importance took place, and when a captain died in battle they went so far as to
suspend combat in order hold funerary athletic games [Sabbatucci, 1998;
Riemschneider, 1997].

## The agonistic state of mind

An agonistic state of mind is defined by situations in which conflicts have
been defused and their place has been taken by contests or competitions.
Sports are a prime example of this; they are widespread and exist in many
different types or disciplines. However, the agonistic state of mind is not
merely an aspect of recreation, but is a regular and important part of politics, economics and culture. In these contexts it is necessary for rivals to

behave as adversaries, and not as enemies. When violence and hostility are eliminated from the very beginning, there remains the possibility of winning or of overcoming the competitor according to rules established in advance [Freund, 1995].

The balance of the agonistic state of mind is dynamic, and disruptive factors can put this balance in jeopardy at any moment. On the other hand, the attempt to create stability through the implementation of too many rules and regulations can bring about the opposite effect and cause the agonistic state of mind to degenerate into pure violence. In this sense, an agonistic state of mind excludes stable equilibrium, as it must inevitably be dynamic and unstable. The results of competition derive from the meeting of opposing, heterogeneous and unpredictable forces and movements which can be neutralized but are never cancelled out.

In short, we are always playing, competing or vying for something, but not only for the material stakes of the competition. It is in fact the immaterial result that is absolutely fundamental: the victory. Victory brings satisfaction, esteem and honour. This shows that competition is not ultimately focused on the mere wish for power or for control over others, but above all on the aspiration to surpass others, the desire to be honoured, esteemed: in brief, the desire to triumph.

One always competes, challenges oneself, or fights *in* something: in strength, in knowledge, in skill; but also *with* something: with the body, intellect, weapons, or words. In archaic societies, where knowledge was regarded as magic or sacred, the most widespread form of competition was based on wisdom and knowledge. This was especially emphasized in sacred festivals, in which individuals competed against each other with words, puzzles and riddles. The spirit of competition served the function of promoting personal courage and heroism, and thus of furthering the development of the civilization's social life. In this way, if the nobility was inspired by honour and courage, these virtues — when they could not be used in war — were made part of an idealized rivalry and transformed into the unwritten codes of honour that governed social interaction and even religion: one need only think of the world of the samurai in which the sense of duty and of rules permeated every aspect society [Yamamoto, 2002].

The ritualization of harmful conflicts is one of the fundamental processes of the biological and cultural evolution of human beings. Verbal competition, which represents an extreme ritualization of agonistic behaviour, creates the possibility of transferring conflicts from the physical arena to that of language and contributes, in a decisive way, to making human existence peaceful and harmonious. Studies of this subject show that there are cross-cultural constants among the strategies use in verbal competition (including delegitimization, accusation, defamation, slander, etc.) which represent some of the rules of conduct upon which strategies of social interaction are structured.

In conclusion, since the first phases of life on earth, competition has been the most important factor in the transformation, selection and adaptation of species. The extraordinary diversity of life finds its *unitas multiplex* in the evolutionary process. Without entering into the debate between the supporters of a rigorous determinism [Dawkins, 1976] and the supporters of the principle of chance [Gould, 2002] it is possible to affirm that in the next few years this will be one of the dilemmas to which science will have to expound a comprehensive response. Life expresses itself through biological functions of a very high complexity, it also does so through history and culture. Moreover, the life that exists now is not the life that always was; and the life that was before does not always exist today, and this shows the variability of life in every one of its categories.

According to von Bertalanffy,

( . . . ) from a biological point of view, life does not consist of maintaining or restoring balance, but essentially of the maintenance of imbalances, in such a way as is revealed by the doctrine of the organism understood as an open system. The search for balance means death and decline. Psychologically, behaviour is not aimed only at easing tensions, but also at building them; if this tendency stops, the subject becomes a mental body in decline, in the same way that a live organism becomes a body in decline when the tensions and the forces which draw it way from balance disappear. [1983: 196]

This great scientist showed the inadequacy of the notions of balance and of homeostasis as part of the ideology of the "living machine". The identity of human beings cannot be likened to a point in balance. Our identity instead consists in the dynamic unfolding of a series of processes the objective of which is precisely to unsettle a state of balance. The myth of the "egoistic gene" has little to do with the evolution of the species. In other words, human behaviour is not governed exclusively by utilitarian principles directed at individual adaptation and the survival of the species. The great creations of human culture, whether they issued from God, from pure chance or from pre-existing psychological laws, are born of a deep sense and understanding of past human experiences. It is in those past experiences that the greatest enigma resides. It is there that we, created beings and creators at the same time, will find the key for drawing nearer to the secret of our origins.

# The Cognition of Happiness

In recent decades investigators from outside the traditional anthropological-philosophical domains have considered the nature of happiness, and the question has thus become part of new and different disciplinary territories. The term happiness and its equivalents (Italian *felicità*, German *Heiterkeit*) refer to an intensely positive subjective state. As a (more or less stable) condition of complete satisfaction, the notion of happiness occupies a prominent place in the moral doctrines of classical antiquity. The Greeks indicated this condition with the term *eudaimonía*, which is a synonym for happiness. In reality, the concept of happiness, as a condition of fullness of being, is different according to different philosophies, visions of the world, and characteristics of the individual who experiences happiness (serenity, contentment, excitement, optimism, freedom from any need, and so on). From the beginning human beings have sought corporeal sensations and intellectual emotions that bring them well-being and joy for moments and longer periods of their lives. When human beings reach such a condition, they achieve satisfaction and contentment [Oatley, 2007].

Analyzed from the point of view of the necessities of life (primary, secondary, etc.), there are definitions of happiness which are different not only from the point of view of psychology and philosophy, but also in material terms. Happiness has its foundation in the satisfaction of primary necessities which derive from biological instincts and impulses, such as hunger, sleep, sexual gratification and still more [Haidt, 2007].

Naturally the satisfaction of biological instincts and impulses can be considered as an integral part of happiness [Haidt, 2007], but not as its exclusive constituents. Biological necessities create a condition of expectation and of unhappiness which tends to be resolved in the moment these needs are satisfied. This satisfaction generates a "biological happiness", identifiable with pleasure, which inevitably influences the mind, although this condition is always changeable as the same impulses and instincts will certainly arise again. In the *psychology of economics*, the decline of the theory that a rise in income increases individual well-being led to the birth of several theories, including that called the *paradox of happiness*. According to Easterlin [1974], happiness does not derive so much from the possession of material goods as from the capacity to develop relational values, or, if one wishes, from the capacity to generate goods the value of which is defined by a relationship among people. It must be said that the interest of scientific psychology in happiness is rather recent, and followed the abandonment of mind-body dualism, which assigned pleasures to the body and the intellectual virtue of happiness to the spirit. It was necessary for the mind to re-enter "legitimate" scientific research programs before happiness could be investigated from a psychological point of view [Legrenzi, 1998]. Thereupon the realization soon followed that the categories of well-being, ecstasy and still others — to which, in the past, the term of happiness was applied — are states of mind that are very different one from another [Argyle, 1988].

Now, if happiness for psychologists corresponds with a state of mind, with a general sensation of pleasure and satisfaction, for economists it corresponds instead with the satisfaction of desires and preferences. Therefore, what must be pragmatically investigated is the desirability and not the utility of an object, which is tied to the pleasure that the object produces. Abandoning the *hedonic* notion of utility not only brings the centre of attention back to subjective states such as satisfaction, pain, pleasure, and so on, but also lays the basis for their observation and, in some cases, for their measurement [Argyle, 1999]. Many psychological studies have highlighted the importance of personal relationships to individual well-being. The most significant results reported are that

(a)  interpersonal relationships are spontaneous between human beings and are sought out in order to improve personal well-being. The presence of these motivations, beginning at an early age, shows that the search for human relationships has in instinctual foundation;
(b)  being deprived of these relationships leads to malaise, sometimes even to sickness; and
(c)  the adaptation to positive or negative events is decidedly partial .

In recent years economists have tried to "measure" the happiness of people by comparing it with some typical economic indicators such as income, wealth, unemployment and so on. In 1971, Brickman and Campbell, extending adaptation theory to the study of individual and collective happiness, came to the conclusion that happiness follows the adaptation (or *set point*) theory, according to which improvements in the objective circumstances of life (income and wealth included) *do not produce real effects on the well-being of individuals*. In fact, one can witness a growing trend toward satisfaction with one's life in individuals with lower income levels.

Recently Blanchard [2005] published a "dispersion diagram" which relates per capita income to an average index of self-declared well-being for a large number of countries in the world. This diagram highlights the fact that the inhabitants of countries with higher levels of income do not declare themselves to be particularly happy, but rather provide ambiguous results. Individuals who double their income do not double their happiness [Inglehart et al., 2008], as the maximum benefit deriving from newly acquired happiness diminishes with time and people set themselves higher and higher objectives. The studies carried out by Inglehart revealed how individuals plot out unique paths in search of their own happiness, disproving the thesis of biologists according to whom it is possible to trace happiness back to a genetic predisposition, and supporting, on the contrary, the determining role of life conditions. When the needs directly linked to survival are satisfied, for example, they gradually receive less and less attention compared to non-physiological necessities. From the moment an individual's level of income or resources frees him/her from the problem of survival, individual happiness no longer depends in any important way on further increases in income, but rather on the quality of life and on the possibilities for self-expression.

Defining one's own value on the basis of money and material possessions corresponds with inferior levels of happiness, a sort of "zero-sum game" in which the constant need to improve oneself and to receive approval serves only to create and perpetuate a vicious cycle of consumption. More recently, the psychologist Csíkszentmihályi [2007] pointed out another variable that has nothing to do with wealth, which he calls *flow* or "optimal experience", maintaining that a deep and stable sense of happiness can come about when one concentrates on and works hard at the achievement of an important objective (which is especially the case in creative endeavours), and finally succeeds in reaching that objective. The American psychologist Seligman [2003] actually proposes a formula for happiness:

$$H = S + C + V$$

in which H stands for *happiness* or rather our permanent level of happiness; S stands for *set range* or of happiness, depending on one's outlook on life; C indicates the circumstances of our life which can influence the level of happiness (wealth/poverty, marriage, social life, age, health, sex, faith, etc.); and V indicates all those factors which depend upon our voluntary control. According to Seligman the first two factors S and C are impossible or difficult to change, while it is possible to work on many internal circumstances (V) in order to increase our permanent level of happiness; among these circumstances are positive emotions which can relate to the past, the present and the future.

# A paradoxical happiness

Around the middle of the 1970s Richard Easterlin restarted the debate on individual happiness with his description of the *paradox of happiness*. The evidence reported by Easterlin suggested that over the course of a lifetime, people's happiness depends very little on variations in income or wealth. Even comparisons between different countries did not show significant correlations between income and happiness: poorer countries did not show higher indexes of "unhappiness" compared to richer countries. The evidence reported by Easterlin had very important consequences: not only did it contribute to modifying the idea according to which the well-being of a nation is measured by indexes of macroeconomic growth, but it also urged economists and psychologists to investigate more thoroughly the causes of happiness itself. The important question naturally arises: if it is not economic success that guarantees a "happy" life, then what are the determining forces of individual and social well-being?

Easterlin, like Kahneman, Frank and others, tried to explain this paradox by using the metaphor of the so-called "treadmill effect", according to which an increase in income/wealth leads to an effect similar to that produced by running on a treadmill, that is, of little forward movement. The principal effects are:

(1) *hedonic*, according to which our satisfaction or well-being subsequent to the acquisition of a new consumer good, after a temporary improvement, regresses to its previous level;
(2) *satisfying*, according to which, when one's income rises, in order that objective happiness may increase, continuous and more intense pleasures are necessary; and
(3) *situational*, on the basis of which the well-being that we draw from consumption depends above all on the value of the consumption itself as compared with the consumption of others.

It is interesting that when one's income increases an individual needs continuous and more intense pleasures in order to maintain the same level of satisfaction. The *satisfaction treadmill effect* shows how subjective happiness remains constant despite marked improvements in the material conditions of life [Easterlin, 2001]. In the domain of material goods, the phenomenon of adaptation is almost universal: after a more or less short amount of time the increase in comfort supplied by a new object is almost completely "absorbed" and forgotten. Because of hedonic adaptation and social competition individuals are not able to perceive that their aspirations of reaching certain levels of monetary earnings are out of touch with real life circumstances. Consequently, a large amount of time is used in the pursuit of earnings that not only work to the disadvantage of family life and health, but also progressively reduce subjective well-being [Kahneman, 2004]. Instead, dedicating time to family life and to health increases subjective well-being [Easterlin, 2001]. An explanation for the paradox which is widely accepted by economists places emphasis on the so-called *situational effects*. In other words, the well-being deriving from consumption depends above all on the relative value of the consumption itself, that is, on the effects deriving from a comparison between our consumption and that of others. It follows that the perception of happiness is influenced by three elements:

(a) *adaptation* (according to *adaptation theory*), in which the pleasure brought about by a new good or by a position that has been reached gradually fades away;
(b) *satisfaction*, according to which, once a certain standard of life has been reached, one's objectives are projected towards pleasures which are progressively more intense; and
(c) *relational competition*, in which one's perception of having acquired or achieved an element of happiness is invalidated by a comparison between one's own position and that of the community in which one coexists.

## Happiness according to Kahneman

With a re-interpretation of the Benthamian concept of utility, according to which utility is linked to any object or action able to diminish or increase happiness, Kahneman advanced his idea of a *hedonic psychology* [Kahneman, Diener and Schwarz, 1999]. As we saw previously, in Bentham's vision utility is the capacity of a given object to produce benefit, pleasure, happiness; or, vice versa, to prevent pain, bad things or unhappiness from happening. In *An Introduction to the Principles of Morals and Legislation*, Bentham writes:

> Nature has placed mankind under the governance of two sovereign masters, pain and pleasure. It is for them alone to point out what we ought to do, as well as to determine what we shall do ( . . . ). In words a man may pretend to abjure their empire: but in reality he will remain subject to it all the while. The principle of utility recognises this subjection, and assumes it for the foundation of that system, the object of which is to rear the fabric of felicity by the hands of reason and of law. [Bentham, 1948, pp. 1–2]

According to Bentham it is possible to construct a scientific system — a sort of felicific calculus — which measures pleasure and pain through categories such as quality, intensity, duration and certainty. An action that generates happiness is useful, and this happiness increases the happiness of one's community. According to Viale [2005] it is necessary to distinguish between two forms of utility: the decision utility of a result, namely the weight assigned to the result in a decision; and the experienced utility of a result, that is the measurement of the hedonic experience of the outcome produced. The distinction between these two types of utility opens up new paths in the study of rationality and decision making, and in evaluating the degree of happiness that a certain choice produces [Seligman and Csikszentmihalyi, 2000].

In reality it rarely happens that the expected utility is maximized, and therefore attempts to reach high and stable levels of pleasure are almost always destined to fail. Moreover, errors in the attribution of decision utility to obtained results can often issue from incorrect predictions of hedonic experience [Bruni and Porta, 2004]. In particular, the evaluation of our past hedonic experiences can undergo important variations and thus lead to error. This is because hedonic experience can change in relation to different circumstances and can also change with time. Also for this reason it is particularly difficult to specify what we will like in the future and therefore to create an accurate expected utility. Very often we are not able to predict our hedonic responses to external stimuli. Even when we find ourselves in situations that allow for the formulation of precise predictions we tend to decide on our future consumption without considering the changeability of our preferences. But it is above all retrospective evaluation that characterizes the formation of hedonic utility; retrospective evaluation represents the sum of knowledge that an individual has accumulated in relation to stimuli and events. If it is true that in our life we rely on memory to guide our future choices, it is also true that even when it seems very reliable, memory can prove misleading. Let us now take a closer look at this issue.

## Illusions and disillusions of memory

The unreliability of memory derives from the fact that the elements of each experience are so disparate that with the distance of time, the reconstruction of an event becomes difficult [Oliverio, 2008]. Memories do not depend on a single "trace", but depend on the complex task of recomposing the "fragments" of different autobiographical levels. Just as single memories depend on the reconstruction of a mosaic composed of different materials (visual, auditory, and olfactory perceptions, semantic criteria and still more), so the memories of our life depend on the reuniting of heterogeneous fragments.

This conception of the autobiographical memory is corroborated by obser-vations of patients afflicted with forms of *retrograde amnesia* which have "erased" fragments of their past. These patients, while generally conserving their long-term memory, lose their memories of specific events or of more recent years. In order to reconstruct their own past, amnesiac patients, when they see family members (almost as though it were the first time), must "insert" the specific facts of their past and of more recent general events into the story line of their own autobiographical memory. The biographical elements learned from others are experienced with cold detachment, even if they contribute to the reconstruction of autobiographical continuity, and more broadly to the meaning of the patient's existence. A person who has lost part of his/her memory collects the new information and uses it on order to "tell him/herself stories" about his/her own identity. In truth, all of us tell ourselves stories about our past and progressively restructure the meaning of single memories, to the point where the reality of memory becomes progressively less important compared to its reconstruction "in parts" which implies distortions, embellishments, omissions, transforma-tions and so on.

With the passing of time numerous details and specific events can become more ambiguous and slowly be modified in our memories. In order to investigate this phenomenon, studies were carried out in which volun-teers had to note down in a diary important events of their everyday life. Some time later a psychologist read back passages from their diaries to the volunteers, asking if they remembered the events recorded. In some cases the psychologist deliberately modified the (typewritten) text: the longer the interval of time that had elapsed, the higher the probability was that the volunteers would recognize the (false) events described in "their" diary as their own memories. The inability to grasp the difference between one's own "true" and "false" memories depends, in large part, on the oblivion that autobiographical memory faces.

The studies of Marigold Linton very clearly demonstrate the prevalence and thus the importance of this phenomenon. In 1972, the American psychologist began to note down in a diary various everyday events in a concise manner. In order to avoid allotting different space to different memories, which might facilitate the recollection of some memories instead of others, she noted events day by day, standardizing the annotations in length to about three lines each. Linton wrote down at least two events per day, and once a month she randomly reviewed the pages relating to two days, re-read them, and tried to establish the date on which they had occurred and to recall the events. At the moment the events were noted down and upon their re-reading they were also evaluated in terms of impor-tance, meaning, the emotions involved, etc. Through this technique, which allowed her to be both an experimental subject and an experimental object at the same time, Linton was able to establish that memory vanishes at the rate of approximately 5–6 per cent per year. This rate would entail the disappearance of about half of the memories of specific events after thirteen years if these were not held within a wider system of autobiographical memory containing general facts and data about the periods of our life. These wider systems of memory are made up of single elements which can in fact disintegrate, while the perception of the general structure and meaning of memories remains [Oliverio, 1998]. Another aspect of autobiographical memories is our ability to date them with some measure of precision. Generally, we have the sensation that particular events have happened more frequently the better our memory of them is. For this reason more recent events are both dated with greater precision and are considered to be more frequent, while events that are further away in time are dated in an approximate way and are held to be rarer than they actually were. A large number of our errors in dating derive from the fact that our interior perception of time does not coincide with real time: if we are active and involved in a number of activities, events that are relatively close to us in time seem more distant, while the opposite happens when we are inactive or not very busy.

One of the mechanisms that regulates the dating precision of our memories is the association between individual memories and collective points of reference. For example, we can easily recall something that happened to us "at the time when", "the day that", "the year in which" a particularly memorable event occurred. When these points of reference are lacking, our dating of memories can be very imprecise, which contributes to the lessening of the accuracy of the memories themselves, to the extent that we may be unsure whether some events occurred or not [Oliverio, 1998]. It must be said that memory is often imagined as an file in which experiences are deposited, a durable file which contains the so-called long-term memories, consolidated and stabilized on the basis of short-term or working memories. This two-tiered conception of memory was established as a result of the theories of Donald O. Hebb [1904–1985], who was the first to maintain that short-term memory depended on electrical alterations of the synapses while long-term memory depended on structural alterations. In accordance with Hebbian theories, psychobiologists demonstrated that the process of memory consolidation was fragile, and that numerous physical treatments — an electric shock given immediately after an experience or the administering of antibiotics which block protein synthesis (and therefore the production of new synapses) — impeded the conversion of short-term memory into long-term memory. However, they maintained that once the consolidation had occurred, nothing was able to disturb stable memories, except for the slow and inexorable process of oblivion, which is more pronounced in older subjects.

Memories, in reality, are not stable, but continuously restructured. Their changeability over time has been demonstrated in two types of research, experimental and clinical. The first approach is based on studies carried out by the psychologist Larry R. Squire [2007] on the effects of electroshock therapy: this treatment — still used by some psychiatrists in cases of serious depression — has a negative effect on human and animal memory. If this treatment is administered immediately after an experience, specifically before short-term memory has been transformed into long-term memory, retrograde amnesia occurs, erasing the memory of that experience. The reason for this is that electroshocks disturb the electrical phenomena that form short-term memory, thereby impeding its consolidation. Squire, however, pointed out that electroshock acts not only on the consolidation of memory, that is on the transformation of short-term memory into long-term memory, but also on the memories that have already been consolidated. This contradicts to some extent the established dogma that memory, once consolidated, could no longer be disrupted by treatments that disturb the electrical phenomena at the basis of short-term memory. If what Squire found is true, the stability of long-term memory would be a myth and the process of its consolidation would not ensure the retention of the experiences codified in a "stable" form. Some recent research linked to the studies of Karin Nader [2003], Joseph LeDoux [2002] and Susan Sara and Jean Przybyslawski [1997] tends to corroborate Squires findings and demonstrates that in addition to consolidation, re-consolidation also exists, which is the re-structuring of previous experiences.

A particular type of restructuring permits the incorporation of false memories into the long-term memory of subjects who have been shown doctored photographs: cognitive psychologists explained that when the false images refer to infancy they can generate false memories which are incorporated in the subject's autobiographical memory and convince the individual that a certain event really did happen. Images, in fact, can be more deceiving than words, which is shown by the frequent use of more than one story in attempts to implant a false memory in a person's mind.

## Happiness and temporality

Cognitive psychologists maintain that in order to effectively evaluate an event retrospectively it is necessary to:

(a)  recall the experiences of the moment that gave rise to that event;
(b)  try to understand the instantaneous perceptions and sensations; and
(c)  express a global evaluation.

In order to perform these operations various procedures exist. One may invoke the principle of *temporal integration* according to which states of mind that follow one after another in time must be treated in the same way. Even more effective than temporal integration is the principle of *temporal monotonicity*, which means that in a sequence of experiences, if one element is made more pleasurable, the whole new sequence will be preferred, but if one element is made less pleasurable, the initial sequence will be preferred [Viale, 2005].

Numerous studies have shown, however, that actual retrospective evaluations involve neither the use of the *principle of temporal integration* nor that of *temporal monotonicity*. When performing a comprehensive assessment individuals use rules such as that of *peak-end* [Redelmeier and Kahneman, 1996], according to which, through consideration of a combination of the most intense effect registered over the course of the entire event and of the sensation occurring in the final phase, global evaluations can be made with a high rate of precision. Another rule is that of *indifference or insensitivity to duration*: the global retrospective evaluation of pain or pleasure is not influenced by the duration of the event.

Here is an example of experimentally demonstrated violations to the law of *temporal monotonicity*. Some paid volunteers who had been divided into two groups were led to believe that they would be subjected to three experiments causing moderate physical pain, while in reality there were only two such experiments. In the "short trial" the subject had to keep one of his/her hands immersed in 14°C water for sixty seconds, drying it off immediately afterwards. In the "long trial" the subject had to keep his/her other hand immersed for ninety seconds: for the first sixty seconds the temperature of the water was kept at 14°C, exactly as in the "short trial"; but during the following thirty seconds the temperature of the water was gradually increased to 15°C, a level that was still unpleasant but perceived by the majority as being a clear improvement compared to the beginning. The first group was subjected first to the short trial and then to the long, while for the second group the order was reversed. A few minutes after the conclusion of the second trial the participants were reminded that they still had to face a third experiment. They were then asked which of the two trials just experienced they would choose to repeat. The choices of the trial to be repeated were clearly different in the two groups. In the first group 17 out of 21 preferred to repeat the long trial, violating the principle of *temporal monotonicity*; in the second group, only 5 out of 11 expressed that preference. The results of both groups satisfied the *peak-end rule*, confirming the indifference towards duration. For a minority composed of individuals who did not feel any decrease in discomfort, the *peak* and *end* levels of pleasure were the same in both the short and the long trial. These subjects should have given the same evaluation to the two trials in accordance with the *peak-end rule*, a prediction confirmed by the distribution of the real preferences close to the

50 per cent mark. In the case of the larger group of subjects who indicated a decrease in discomfort in the final phase of the long trial, according to the *peak-end rule* this experiment should have caused less aversion than the short trial, and this prediction was also confirmed by their real choices. In all, about two thirds of the subjects in this experiment violated the principle of dominance, a result confirmed by numerous experiments carried out on a wide range of individuals in a series of slightly different conditions.

Further analyses have clarified the mechanism responsible for these violations of *temporal monotonicity*. The majority of the subjects convinced themselves, erroneously, that the lowest temperature to which they had been exposed had not been the same in the two trials, as their memory of the worst moment of the long trial had been softened by the improvement that occurred in the final phase. The evidence suggests that events are judged more through a few snapshots of the experience rather than through a continuous recollection of the experience similar to a film clip. The snapshots are, in effect, montages that can blend impressions drawn from various parts of the experience. The whole experience is evaluated on the basis of the weighted average of the utility of these moments [Viale, 2005].

As we have seen, there are many variables which make the measurement of happiness or, as Kahneman says, of "subjective well-being", extremely difficult. Among other things, one would need to decide whether to adopt a *bottom-up* analysis, which would be based on the assumption that it is the circumstances or the environment that determines greater or lesser happiness, or a *top-down* analysis, which would be based on the assumption that it is personality that constitutes the strongest determining factor of well-being, and overall happiness influences the sentiments that are felt in different situations. On the other hand, unhappiness is also of great interest. Legrenzi [1998] considers unhappiness not the opposite of happiness, but the result of the activation of specific human cognitive mechanisms. In his attempt to give an account of unhappiness Kahneman [Kahneman, Diener and Schwarz, 1999] takes various explanatory levels into consideration. The first level is the social and cultural context that the subject is part of. Secondly, there are the objective characteristics of the society in which the subject lives (poverty, infant mortality, social unrest, and so on); Kahneman places less emphasis on the balance of pleasure or pain or subjective affirmations, which however remain important. Subjective well-being involves a component of judgement and of comparison with ideals, aspirations, others and one's own past. Global well-being is strongly correlated with a series of emotional states, with their persistence and with their connection to particular events; and here the individual differences are very noteworthy. Third and finally, there are the neuronal and motivational systems that may cause unhappiness.

Here, as often, in order to understand the higher levels it is necessary to understand the lower ones. Kahneman [Kahneman, Diener and Schwarz, 1999] developed a system for evaluating happiness from the bottom up, and introduced a new concept, the *Good/Bad* dimension, a general dimension for evaluating happiness. He first of all distinguishes four variants of *G/B*, which are differentiated by the level of integration to which they refer:

- *happiness, well-being*: dimensions at the highest level of integration that pertain to all areas of life;
- *satisfaction*: which refers to wider areas of life, such as family life or work;
- *remembered utility*: the global evaluation assigned to a particular past event or to a situation in which a similar experience recurs; and
- *instant utility*: that is to say satisfaction or dissatisfaction as attributes of an experience at a particular moment. This constitutes the most useful category for understanding the predisposition for wanting to stop or continue an experience in progress.

In order to identify objective and normative criteria which would allow us to understand happiness, Kahneman uses a bottom-up analysis which proceeds from the bottom (*instant utility*) towards the top. This involves the elimination of the subjective judgements that an individual formulates about his/her own state. In other words, first he admits the role of subjectivity in the evaluation of *instant utility*, and then he abandons it, as the retrospective evaluation of an event can be influenced by errors in memory or by emotions. Subjective evaluations can in fact be highly influenced by emotional experiences. It follows that an individual who has had experiences the majority of which are negative will, in all probability, describe him/herself as unsatisfied or unhappy.

Kahneman [2007] distinguishes between objective and subjective happiness: the first derives from the registration of *instant utility* during a certain event; the second is reflected in the answer tothe question of how happy a person is. The relationship between objective and subjective happiness is analogous to the relationship between the total utility and the remembered utility of an event. Paradoxically, in the end objective happiness is based on subjective data: the *G/B* experiences of moments in life. It has been called objective because the summation of instantaneous utilities is determined by logical rules and could in theory be performed by an observer who has access to the temporal data on instant utility. A human being's natural inclination is to define the total utility felt during a period of time as the temporal sum of instant utility. Kahneman attempts to describe the procedures necessary for this method by invoking some principles regarding subjective assessments. First of all, assessments must contain all of the useful and relevant elements in order to allow for temporal integration. Second, the scale has a stable zero point (which corresponds with *neither pleasant nor unpleasant, neither approach nor avoid*), and the measurements of the decisions that diverge from this point are measurable. Third, subjective evaluations must correctly rate experiences on the basis of their *good/bad* intensity, but the intervals between the assessments can be arbitrary. And fourth, the observer must have knowledge of the points of reference used by the subject. These assumptions, however, relate to a theoretical possibility rather than a practical procedure.

These considerations highlight just how difficult it is, on the basis of our past experiences, to predict what we will desire in the future, given the fact that our reactions to similar stimuli change with time and in relation to the circumstances [Stutzer and Frey, 2006]. Predicting which choices will make us happy is very difficult, but the stream of studies regarding the *economy of happiness* is trying, even in the face of many problems, to give us an explanation of how the "search" for happiness works.

# Bibliography

ALIPRANTIS C. D., CHAKRABARTI S. K. (2000) *Games and decision making*. Oxford University Press, New York.

ALLAIS M. (1953) "Le comportement de l'homme rationnel devant le risque: critique des postulats et axiomes de l'école américaine". In *Econometrica*, 21, pp. 503–546.

ARGYLE M. (1988) *Psicologia della felicità*. Cortina, Milan.

ARGYLE M. (1994) *The psychology of social class*. Routledge, London.

ARGYLE M. (1999) "Causes and correlates of happiness". In Kahneman D., Diener E., Schwarz N. (eds.) *Well-Being: the foundations of hedonic psychology*. Russell Sage Foundation, New York, pp. 353–374.

ARISTOTLE (1973) *Nicomachean Ethics* in *Introduction to Aristotle*, Edited with a General Introduction and Introductions to the Particular Works by Richard McKeon. Trans. W. D. Ross, The University of Chicago Press, Chicago and London.

ARKES H. R., AYTON P. (1999) "The sunk cost and Concorde effects: are humans less rational than lower animals?". In *Psychological bulletin*, 125, pp. 591–600.

ARKES H. R., BLUMER C. (1985) "The psychology of sunk cost". In *Organizational behavior and human decision processes*, 35, pp. 124–140.

AXELROD R. (1984) *The evolution of cooperation*. Basic Books, New York. Tr. it. (1985) *Giochi di reciprocità. L'insorgenza della cooperazione*. Feltrinelli, Milan.

BARBERIS N., THALER R. (2003) "A survey of behavioral finance". In Constantinides G. M., Harris M., Stulz R. M. (eds.) *Handbook of the economics of finance*. Elsevier/North-Holland, Boston, MA, pp. 1051–1121.

BAYES T. (1763) "Essay towards solving a problem in the doctrine of chances". In *Philosophical transactions of the royal society of london*, 53, pp. 370–418.

BECHARA A., DAMASIO A. R., DAMASIO H., TRANEL D. (1997) "Deciding advantageously before knowing the advantageous strategy". In *Science*, 275 (5304), pp. 1293–1295.

BECHARA A., DAMASIO H., DAMASIO A. R. (2000) "Emotion, decision making, and the orbitofrontal cortex". In *Cerebral cortex*, 10, n. 3, pp. 295–307.

BENCIVENGA E. (1985) *Il primo libro di logica. Introduzione alla logica contemporanea*. Bollati Boringhieri, Turin.

BENTHAM J. (1948) *The principles of morals and legislation*. Hafner Publishing Company Inc., Darien, CT.

BENTHAM J. (1988) *Collected works of Jeremy Bentham*. Vol. 8, Bertrams, New York.

BERNOULLI D. (1738) "Specimen theoriae novae de mensura sortis". In *Commentarii academiae scientiarum imperialis Petropolitanae*, 5, pp. 175–192.

BERNOULLI D. (1954/1738) "Exposition of a new theory on the measurement of risk". In *Econometrica*, 22 (1), pp. 23–36.

BERNS G. S., McCLURE S. M., PAGNONI G., MONTAGUE P. R. (2001) "Predictability modulates human brain response to reward". In *Journal of neuroscience*, 21, pp. 2793–2798.

BERTALANFFY VON L. (1983) *Teoria generale dei sistemi*. Mondadori, Milan.

BERTHOZ A. (2006) *Emotion and reason; the cognitive science of decision making*. Trans. Giselle Weiss. Oxford University Press, Oxford.

BERTO F. (2008) *Tutti pazzi per Gödel!* Laterza, Rome-Bari.

BERTUGLIA C. S., VAIO F. (2003) *Non linearità, caos, complessità: le dinamiche dei sistemi naturali e sociali*. Bollati Boringhieri, Turin.

BETTMAN J. R. (1993) "The decision maker who came in from the cold". In McAlister L., Rothschild M. (eds.) *Advances in consumer research*, 10, pp. 7–11.

BLANCHARD O. (2005) *Macroeconomics*. Prentice Hall, New Jersey.

BOELLA L. (2008) *Neuroetica. La morale prima della morale*. Raffaello Cortina, Milan.

BOYD R., LORBERBAUM J. P. (1987) "No pure strategy is evolutionarily stable in the repeated prisoner's dilemma game". In *Nature*, 327, pp. 58–59.

BRAINE M. D. S. (1978) "On the relation between the natural logic of reasoning and standard logic". In *Psychological review*, 85, pp. 1–21.

BRAUN P. A., YANIV A. (1992) "A case study of expert judgment. Economists' probabilities versus base-rate model forecasts". In *Journal of behavioral decision making*, 5, pp. 217–231.

BRICKMAN P., CAMPBELL D. T. (1971) "Hedonic relativism and planning the good society". In Apley M. H. (ed.) *Adaptation-level theory: a symposium*. Academic Press, New York, pp. 287–302.

BROSNAN S. F., DE WAAL F. B. M. (2003) "Monkeys reject unequal pay". In *Nature*, 425, pp. 297–299.

BRUNI L., PORTA P. L. (2004) *Felicità ed economia*. Guerini & Associati, Milan.

BUCCINO G. et al. (2004) "Neural circuits underlying imitation learning of hand actions: an event related fMRI study". In *Neuron*, 42, pp. 323–334.

BYRNE R. M. J. (2005) *The rational imagination*. Bradford, MIT Press, Cambridge, MA.

BYRNE R. M. J., TASSO A. (1999) "Deductive reasoning with factual, possible and counterfactual conditionals". In *Memory and cognition*, 27, pp. 726–740.

CAMERER C. F., FEHR E. (2006) "When does 'economic' man dominate social behavior?". In *Science*, 311, pp. 47–52.

CAMERER C. F., LOEWENSTEIN G., PRELEC D. (2004) "Neuroeconomia, ovvero come le neuroscienze possono dare una nuova forma all'economia". In *Sistemi intelligenti*, 3, pp. 337–418.

CAMERER C. F., THALER R. H. (1995) "Anomalies. Ultimatums, dictators and manners". In *Journal of economic perspectives*, 9, pp. 209–219.

CANOLTY R. T., EDWARDS E., DALAL S. S., SOLTANI M., NAGARAJAN S. S., KIRSCH

H. E., BERGER M. S., BARBARO N. M., KNIGHT R. T., (2006) "High gamma power is phase-locked to theta oscillations in human neocortex". In *Science*, 313 (5793), pp. 1626–8.

CHOMSKY N. (1957) *Syntactic structures*. The Hague, Mouton.

CHOMSKY N. (2000) *On nature and language*. Cambridge University Press, New York.

CHORVAT T., McCABE K., SMITH V. (2004) "Law and neuroeconomics". In *Law and economics working paper series*. George Mason University, Fairfax, Virginia.

CIOMPI L. (1994) *Logica affettiva*. Feltrinelli, Milan.

CODARA L. (1998) *Le mappe cognitive*. Carocci, Rome.

CORICELLI G. G., CRITCHLEY H. D., JOFFILY M. M., O'DOHERTY J. P., SIRIGU A., DOLAN R. J. (2005) "Regret and its avoidance, a neuroimaging study of choice behaviour". In *Nature neuroscience*, 8, pp. 1255–1262.

COSMIDES L. (1985) *Deduction or darwinian algorithms? An explanation of the "elusive" content effect on the Wason selection task*. PhD Dissertation, Department of Psychology, Harvard University.

CSÍKSZENTMIHÁLYI M. (2007) *Buon business. Successo economico e comportamento etico*. Il Sole 24 Ore edizioni, Milano.

CZERLINSKI J., GOLDSTEIN D. G., GIGERENZER G. (1999) "How good are simple heuristics?" In Gigerenzer G., Todd P. M. & the ABC Group, *Simple heuristics that make us smart*. Oxford University Press, New York.

DAMASIO A. R. (1994) *Descartes' error: emotion, reason and the human brain*. G. P. Putnam's Sons, New York.

DAMASIO A. R. (1999) *The feeling of what happens: body, emotion and the making of consciousness*. Heinemann, London. Tr. It. (2000), *Emozione e coscienza*. Adelphi, Milan.

DAMASIO A. R. (2003) *Looking for Spinoza*. Harcourt, Inc., New York.

DAMASIO A. R. (2007) "Neuroscience and ethics, intersections". In *American journal of bioethics*, 7, pp. 3–7.

DAMASIO A. R., DAMASIO H., CHRISTEN Y. (1996) *Neurobiology of decision-making*. Springer-Verlag, New York and Berlin.

DAWKINS R. (1976) *The selfish gene*. Oxford University Press, New York. Tr. it. (1996), *Il gene egoista*. Mondadori, Milan.

de QUERVAIN D. J., FISCHBACHER U., TREYER V. et al. (2004) "The neural basis of altruistic punishment". In *Science*, 305, pp. 1254–1258.

DELGADO M. R., FRANK R. H., PHELPS E. A. (2005) "Perceptions of moral character modulate the neural systems of reward during the trust game". In *Nature neuroscience*, 8 (11), pp. 1611–1618.

DELGADO M. R., MILLER M. M., INATI S., PHELPS E. A. (2005) "An fMRI study of reward-related probability learning". In *NeuroImage*, 24 (3), pp. 862–73.

DESCARTES R. (1637) *Discours de la Méthode*. Trans. John Cottingham, Robert Stoothoff and Dugald Murdoch (1985) *Discourse on the Method* in *The Philosophical Writings of Descartes*, Vol. 1. Cambridge University Press, Cambridge.

DOWNS A. (1957) *An economic theory of democracy*. Harper & Row, New York. Tr. it. (1988), *Teoria economica della democrazia*. Il Mulino, Bologna.

DUHEM P. (1954) *The aim and structure of physical theory*. Trans. Philip P. Wiener. Princeton University Press, Princeton, New Jersey.

EASTERLIN R. A. (1974) "Does economic growth improve the human lot?". In P. A. David and M. W. Reder (eds.) *Nations and households in economic growth: essays in honor of Moses Abramovitz*. Academic Press, New York, pages 89–125.

EASTERLIN R. A. (2001) "Income and happiness: towards a unified theory". In *The economic journal*, 111 (473), pp. 465–484.

EDELMAN G. M. (1987) *Neural darwinism: the theory of neuronal group selection*. Basic Books, New York. Tr. it. (1995), *Darwinismo neurale*, Einaudi, Turin.

EDELMAN G. M. (2006) *Brain science and human knowledge*. Yale University Press, New Haven-London.

EDELMAN G. M. (2007) *Seconda natura. Scienza del cervello e conoscenza umana*. Cortina, Milan.

EISER J. R., PLIGT J. VAN DER (1991) *Atteggiamenti e decisioni*. Il Mulino, Bologna.

ELDREDGE N., GOULD S. J. (1972) "Punctuated equilibria: an alternative to phyletic gradualism". In Schops T. J. M. (1972, ed.), *Models in paleobiology*. Freeman, Cooper & Co., San Francisco, pp. 82–115.

ELLIOTT R., NEWMAN J. L., LONGE O. A., DEAKIN J. F. (2003) "Differential response patterns in the striatum and orbitofrontal cortex to financial reward in humans: a parametric functional magnetic resonance imaging study". In *Journal of neuroscience*, 23, pp. 303–307.

ELLSBERG D. (1961) "Risk, ambiguity, and the Savage axioms". In *Quarterly journal of economics*, 75, pp. 643–669.

EVANS J., OVER D. (1997) "Rationality in reasoning: The problem of deductive competence". In *Cahiers de psychologie cognitive*, 16, pp. 102–106.

FRANK R. (1990) "Rethinking rational choice". In Friedland R., Robertson A. (eds.), *Beyond the Marketplace. Rethinking Economy and Society*. Aldine de Gruyter, New York, pp. 53–87.

FREUND J. (1995) *Il 'terzo', il nemico, il conflitto. Materiali per una teoria del politico*. Giuffré, Milan.

FRIJDA N. H. (1986) *The emotions*. Cambridge University Press, Cambridge.

FRIJDA N. H. (1988) "The laws of emotion". In *American psychologist*, 43, pp. 349–358.

FRIJDA N. H. (2000) *The psychologists' point of view*. In Lewis M., Haviland-Jones J. M. (eds., 2nd ed.), *Handbook of emotions*. The Guilford Press, London, pp. 59–74.

FUSTER J. (1997) "Network memory". In *Trends in NeuroScience*, 20 (10), pp. 451–459.

GALLESE V. (2008) "Empathy, embodied simulation and the brain". In *Journal of the american psychoanalytic association*, 56, pp. 769–781.

GAZZANIGA M. S. (1992) *Nature's mind: the biological roots of thinking, emotion, sexuality, language, and intelligence.* Basic Books, New York. Tr. it. (1997), *La mente della natura.* Garzanti, Milan.

GAZZANIGA M. S. (2005) *The ethical brain.* Dana Press, New York/Washington.

GIGERENZER G. (1997) *Bounded rationality: models of fast and frugal inference.* WP, Max Planck Institute for Human Development, Berlin.

GIGERENZER G. (2000) *Adaptive thinking: rationality in the real world.* Oxford University Press, New York.

GIGERENZER G., SELTEN R. (2001) *Bounded rationality: The adaptive toolbox.* The MIT Press, Cambridge, MA.

GIGERENZER G. (2008) *Rationality for mortals: how people cope with uncertainty.* Oxford University Press, New York.

GIGERENZER G. et al. (1999) *Simple heuristics that make us smart.* Oxford University Press, New York.

GIGERENZER G., GOLDSTEIN D. G. (1996) "Reasoning the fast and frugal way: models of bounded rationality". In *Psychological review*, vol. 103, n. 4, pp. 650–669.

GIGERENZER G., SELTEN R. (2001) *Bounded rationality: the adaptive toolbox.* The MIT Press, Cambridge, MA.

GIROTTO V. (1994) *Il ragionamento.* Il Mulino, Bologna.

GIROTTO V. (2004) "Task understanding". In Leighton J. P., Sternberg R. J. (eds.), *The nature of reasoning.* Cambridge University Press, Cambridge, pages 103–128.

GLIMCHER P. W. (2003) *Decisions, uncertainty, and the brain: the science of neuroeconomics.* The MIT Press, Cambridge, MA.

GLIMCHER P. W., RUSTICHINI A. (2004) "Neuroeconomics: the consilience of brain and decision". In *Science*, 306 (5695), pp. 447–452.

GÖDEL K. (1986) *Collected works I: publications 1929–1936.* Feferman S., Kleene S., Moore G., Solovay R., and van Heijenoort J. (eds.), Oxford University Press, Oxford.

GÖDEL K. (1990) *Collected works II: publications 1938–1974.* Feferman S., Dawson J., Leene S., Moore G., Solovay R., and van Heijenoort J. (eds.), Oxford University Press, Oxford.

GOLDSTEIN D. G., GIGERENZER G. (2002) "Models of ecological rationality: the recognition heuristic". In *Psychological review*, 109 (1), pp. 75–90.

GOLEMAN D. (1996) *L'intelligenza emotiva.* Rizzoli, Milan.

GOTTFRIED J. A., O'DOHERTY J., DOLAN R. J. (2003), "Encoding predictive reward value in human amygdala and orbitofrontal cortex". In *Science*, 301 (5636), pp. 1104–1107.

GOULD S. J. (2002) *The structure of evolutionary theory.* Belknap Press, Cambridge, MA.

GOULD S. J. (2008) *L'equilibrio punteggiato.* Codice edizioni. Turin.

GREENE J. D. (2003) "From neural 'is' to moral 'ought': what are the moral implications of neuro-scientific moral psychology?". In *Nature Reviews Neuroscience*, 4, pp. 846–849.

GREENE J. D. et al. (2004) "The neural bases of cognitive conflict and control in moral judgment". In *Neuron*, 44, pp. 389–400.

GREENE J. D., HAIDT J. (2002) "How (and where) does moral judgment work?" In *Trends cognition science*, 6, pp. 517–523.

GREENE J. D., SOMMERVILLE R. B., NYSTROM L. E., DARLEY J. M., COHEN J. D. (2001) "An fMRI investigation of emotional engagement in moral judgment". In *Science*, 293, pp. 2105–2108.

HAIDT J. (2007) *Felicità: un'ipotesi.* Codice edizioni, Turin.

HARSANYI J. C. (1986) *L'utilitarismo.* Il Mulino, Bologna.

HAUSER M. D. (1996) *The evolution of communication.* The MIT Press, Cambridge, MA.

HAUSER M. D. (2006) *Moral minds: how nature designed our universal sense of right and wrong.* Harper Collins, New York. Tr. It. (2007), *Menti Morali. Le origini naturali del bene e del male.* Il Saggiatore, Milan.

HAUSER M. D., CHOMSKY N., FITCH W.T. (2002) "The language faculty: What is it, who has it, and how did it evolve?". In *Science*, 298, 1569–1579.

HAUSER M. D., SPELKE E. (2004) Evolutionary and developmental foundations of human knowledge". In Gazzaniga M. (ed.), *The cognitive neurosciences.* The MIT Press, Cambridge, MA.

HAYEK F. A. (1937) "Economics and knowledge". In *Economica*, 4 (13), pp. 96–105. Reprinted in Hayek F. A. (1949) *Individualism and economic order.* Routledge & Sons, London.

HAYEK F. A. (1963) *The sensory order: an inquiry into the foundations of theoretical psychology.* The University of Chicago Press, Chicago.

HAYEK F. A. (1967) *Studies in philosophy, politics and economics.* Routledge & Kegan Paul, London. Tr. It. (1998), *Studi in filosofia, politica ed economia.* Rubbettino, Soveria-Mannelli.

HAYEK F. A. (1988) *Conoscenza, mercato, pianificazione.* Il Mulino, Bologna.

HAYEK F. A. (1994) *Hayek on Hayek: an autobiographical dialogue.* Edited by Kresge S. and Wenar L. Chicago, University of Chicago Press, Routledge, London.

HEBB D. O. (1949) *The organization of behavior: a neuropsychological theory.* John Wiley Inc., New York.

HEMPEL C. G. (1986) *Aspetti della spiegazione scientifica.* Il Saggiatore, Milan.

HEWSTON M., STROEBE W., STEPHENSON G. M. (1996) *Introduction to social psychology: a European perspective.* Blackwell, Oxford.

HOBBES T. (1994) *The elements of law, natural and politic: part I: human nature; part II: de corpore politico with three lives.* Oxford University Press, Oxford.

HOGART R. M., REDER M. W. (1986) *Rational choice: the contrast between economics and psychology.* The University of Chicago Press, Chicago.

HUME D. (1739) *A treatise on human nature.* London. Tr. it. (1997) *Trattato sulla natura umana.* Bompiani, Milan.

IACOBONI M. (2008) *I neuroni specchio. Come capiamo cosa fanno gli altri.* Bollati Boringhieri, Turin.

INGLEHART R., FOA R., PETERSON C., WELZEL C. (2008) "Development, freedom, and rising happiness: a global perspective (1981–2007)". In *Perspectives on psychological science*, 3 (4), pp. 264–285.

INGRAO B., ISRAEL G. (1990) *The invisible hand: economic equilibrium in the history of science*. The MIT Press, Cambridge, MA.

ISRAEL G. (1992) "L'histoire du principe philosophique du déterminisme et ses rencontres avec les mathématiques". In *Chaos et déterminisme* (Dahan Dalmedico A., Chabert J. L., Chemla K., eds.), Editions du Seuil, Paris, pp. 249–273.

ISRAEL G. (1996) *La mathématisation du réel. Essai sur la modélisation mathématique*. Éditions du Seuil, Paris.

ISRAEL G. (2004) *La macchina vivente. Contro le visioni meccanicistiche dell'uomo*. Bollati Boringhieri, Turin.

JAMES W. (1890) *The principles of psychology*. Dover Publications, New York.

JEVONS W. S. (1871) *The theory of political economy*. Macmillan, London. Tr. It. (1948), *Teoria dell'economia politica*. UTET, Turin.

JOHNSON-LAIRD P. N. (1983) *Mental models: towards a cognitive science of language, inference and consciousness*, Harvard University Press, Cambridge, MA. (trad. it. Bologna 1988).

JOHNSON-LAIRD P.N., LEGRENZI P., GIROTTO V. (2004) "How we detect logical inconsistencies". In *Current directions in psychological science*, 13, pp. 41–45.

KAHNEMAN D. (2000) "Experienced utility and objective happiness". In Kahneman D. and Tversky A. (eds.), *Choices, values and frames*. New York : Cambridge University Press and the Russell Sage Foundation, pp. 673–692.

KAHNEMAN D. (2002) "Maps of bounded rationality: a perspective on intuitive judgment and choice". Prize Lecture, December 8, 2002. Princeton University, Department of Psychology. Princeton, New Jersey.

KAHNEMAN D. (2003) "A perspective on judgment and choice. Mapping bounded rationality". In *American psychologist*, 58, pp. 697–720.

KAHNEMAN D. (2004) "Felicità oggettiva". In Bruni L. and Porta P. L. (eds.), *Felicità ed economia*. Guerini & Associati, Milan.

KAHNEMAN D. (2007) *Economia della felicità*. Il Sole 24 Ore edizioni, Milan.

KAHNEMAN D., DIENER E., SCHWARZ N. (1999) *Well-being: the foundations of hedonic psychology*. Russell Sage Foundation, New York.

KAHNEMAN D., KNETSCH J., THALER R. (1990) "Experimental tests of the endowment effect and the Coase theorem". In *Journal of political economy*, 98 (6), pp. 1325–1348.

KAHNEMAN D., KNETSCH J., THALER R. (1991) "The endowment effect, loss aversion, and status quo bias". In *Journal of economic perspectives*, 5, pages 193–206.

KAHNEMAN D., MILLER, D. T. (1986) "Norm theory: Comparing reality to its alternatives". In *Psychological review*, 93, pp. 136–153.

KAHNEMAN D., RITOV I. (1994) "Determinants of stated willingness to pay for public goods. A study in the headline method". In *Journal of risk and uncertainty*, 9, pp. 5–38.

KAHNEMAN D., SLOVIC P., TVERSKY A. (1982) *Judgment under uncertainty: heuristics and biases*. Cambridge University Press, New York.

KAHNEMAN D., TVERSKY A. (1972), "Subjective probability: a judgment of representativeness". In *Cognitive psychology*, 3, pp. 430–454.

KAHNEMAN D., TVERSKY A. (1973) "On the psychology of prediction". In *Psychological review*, 80, pp. 237–251.

KAHNEMAN D., TVERSKY A. (1979) "Prospect theory: an analysis of decisions under risk". In *Econometrica*, 47, pp. 313–327.

KAHNEMAN D., TVERSKY A. (2000) *Choices, values and frames*. Cambridge University Press, New York.

KANT I. (1781) *Kritik der reinen Vernunft*. Trad. It. (1996) *Critica della ragion pura*. Intr., trad. e note di P. Chiodi, TEA-Utet, Turin.

KENNEDY D. N., NOWINSKI W., THIRUNAVUUKARASUU A. (2003) *Brain atlas for functional imaging*. Thieme Georg Verlag, Berlin, 2003.

KLEIN G. (1998) *Sources of power: how people make decisions*. The MIT Press, Cambridge, MA.

KLEIN G. (2001) "The fiction of optimization". In Gigerenzer G., Selten R. (eds.), *Bounded rationality: the adaptive toolbox*. The MIT Press, Cambridge, MA, pp. 103–121.

KLINE M. (1980) *Mathematics: the loss of certainty*. Oxford University Press, New York.

KNIGHT F. (1960) *Rischio, incertezza e profitto*. La Nuova Italia, Florence.

KOCH C. (2007) *La ricerca della coscienza. Una prospettiva neurobiologica*. UTET, Turin.

KNOCH D., PASCUAL-LEONE A., MEYER K., TREYER V., FEHR E. (2006) "Diminishing reciprocal fairness by disrupting the right prefrontal cortex". In *Science*, 314 (5800), pp. 829 –832.

KNUTSON B., WESTDORP A., KAISER E., HOMMER D. (2000) "FMRI visualization of brain activity during a monetary incentive delay task". In *Neuroimage*, 12, pp. 20–27.

KOENIGS M., YOUNG L., ADOLPHS R. et al. (2007) "Damage to the pre-frontal cortex increases utilitarian moral judgements". In *Nature*, 446, pp. 908–911.

KOSFELD M., HEINRICHS M., ZAK P. J., FISCHBACHER U., FEHR E. (2005) "Oxytocin increases trust in humans". In *Nature*, 435, pp. 673–676.

KRAL V. A., MACLEAN P. D. (1969) *A triune concept of the brain and behaviour, by MacLean P. D. Including Psychology of memory, and Sleep and dreaming, papers presented at Queen's University, Kingston, Ontario, February 1969, by Kral V. A. et al.* Published for the Ontario Mental Health Foundation by Univ. of Toronto Press, Toronto, 1973.

KREPS D. M. (1992) *Teoria dei giochi e modelli economici*. Il Mulino, Bologna.

LAPLACE P.S. (1825) *Essai philosophique sur les probabilités*. Bachelier, Paris. (reprint Paris, Bourgois, 1986, with an introduction by R. Thom).

LAYARD R. (2005) *Happiness: lessons from a new science*. Penguin, New York.

LAZARUS R. S. (1991) *Emotion and adaptation*. Oxford University Press, Oxford, UK.

LAZARUS R. S. (2001) "Relational meaning and discrete emotions". In Scherer K., Schorr A., Johnstone T. (eds.), *Appraisal process in emotion*. Oxford University Press, Oxford, pp. 59–60.

LEDOUX J. (2002) *Il Sé sinaptico. Come il cervello determina la personalità*. Cortina, Milan.

LEGRENZI P. (1998) *Come funziona la mente*. Laterza, Rome-Bari. 1998.

LEGRENZI P. (1998) *La felicità*. Il Mulino, Bologna.

LEGRENZI P., GIROTTO V. (1996) "Mental models in reasoning and decision-making processes". In Oakhill J., Garnham A. (eds.), *Mental models in cognitive science*.. Taylor and Francis, Psychology Press, Hove, Sussex, pp. 95–118.

LEGRENZI P., GIROTTO V., JOHNSON-LAIRD P. N. (1993) "Focusing in reasoning and decision making". In *Cognition*, 49, pp. 37–66.

LEGRENZI P., GIROTTO V., JOHNSON-LAIRD P. N. (2003) "Models of consistency". In *Psychological science*, 14, pp. 131–137.

LEGRENZI P., GIROTTO V., JOHNSON-LAIRD P. N., SONINO M. (2003) "Possibilities and probabilities". In Hardman D. and Macchi L. (eds.), *Reasoning and decision-making*. Wiley, London.

LEGRENZI P., MAZZOCCO A. (1975) *Psicologia del pensiero*. Giunti, Florence.

LEMMON E. J. (2008) *Elementi di logica*. Laterza, Rome-Bari.

LERNER J. S., SMALL, D. A, LOEWENSTEIN G. (2004) "Heart strings and purse strings: carry-over effects of emotions on economic transactions". In *Psychological science*, 15, pp. 337–341.

LEVY B., SERVAN-SCHREIBER E. (1998) *Les secrets de l'intelligence*, (2 CD-ROMs). Édition Hypermind, Ubi Soft, Paris.

LIBET B. (1996) "Brain stimulation and threshold of conscious experience". In Eccles J. C. (ed.), *Brain and conscious experience*. Springer, Berlin, pp. 165–18.

LIBET B. (1999) "Do we have free will?". In *Journal of consciousness studies*, 6 (8–9), pp. 47–57

LINDGREN K. (1991) "Evolutionary phenomena in simple dynamics". In Langton C. G., Taylor C., Farmer J. D., Rasmussen S. (eds.), *Artificial Life II*. Addison-Wesley, Redwood City, pp. 295–312.

LINDLEY D. (1990) *La logica della decisione*. Il Saggiatore, Milan.

LOASBY B. (1976) *Choice, complexity and ignorance*. Cambridge University Press, Cambridge.

LOCKE J. (1960) *An essay concerning human understanding*. Basset, London. Tr. It. (2004), *Saggio sull'intelletto umano*. Bompiani, Milan.

LOEWENSTEIN G. (1996) "Out of control: visceral influences on behavior". In *Organizational behavior and decision processes*, 65, pp. 272–292.

LOLLI G. (2007) *Sotto il segno di Gödel*. Il Mulino, Bologna.

LUCCHETTI R. (2008) *Di duelli, scacchi e dilemmi*. Bruno Mondadori, Milan.

MACLEAN P. D. (1990) *The triune brain in evolution: role in paleocerebral functions*. Plenum Press, New York.

MALDONATO M. (2006) *La mente plurale: biologia, evoluzione, cultura*. Edizioni Universitarie Romane, Rome.

MALDONATO M. (2007) "La coscienza prismatica". In Maldonato M. (ed), *La coscienza: come la biologia inventa la cultura*. Guida, Naples.

MANDEVILLE B. (1714) *The fable of the bees: or, private vices, publick benefits*. London. Tr. it. (2002), *La favola delle api. Ovvero, vizi privati, pubblici benefici con un saggio sulla carità e le scuole di carità e un'indagine sulla natura della società*. Laterza, Rome-Bari.

MARCH J. G. (1994) *A primer on decision making: how decisions happen*. The Free Press, New York. Tr. It. (1998), *Prendere decisioni*. Il Mulino, Bologna.

MARCH J. G., SIMON H. A. (1958) *Organizations*. John Wiley and Sons, New York. Tr. It. (1966), *Teoria delle organizzazioni*. Edizioni di Comunità, Milano.

MARCUS S. (2002) *Neuroethics: mapping the field*. Dana Press, Washington, DC.

MARKOWITZ H. (1952) "Portfolio selection". In *Journal of finance*, 7 (1), pp. 77–91.

MASLOW A. H. (1971) *The farther reaches of human nature*. An Esalen Book/The Viking Press. New York.

McCABE K., HOUSER D., RYAN L., SMITH V., TROUARD T. (2001) "A functional imaging study of cooperation in two-person reciprocal exchange". In *Procedings of the National Academy of Sciences*, 98 (20), pp. 11832–11835.

McFADDEN D. (2005) "Razionalità per economisti?". In Motterlini M., Piattelli Palmarini M., (eds.), *Critica della ragione economica. Tre saggi: Kahneman, McFadden, Smith*. Il Saggiatore, Milan.

MENGER C. (1871) *Grundsätze der Volkswirthschaftslehre*. Wilhelm Braumüller, Vienna. Tr. It. (2001), *Principi di economia politica*. Rubbettino, Soveria Mannelli.

MILLER E. K., COHEN J. D. (2001) "An integrative theory of prefrontal cortex function". In *Annual review of neuroscience*, 24, pp. 167–202.

MIROWSKI P. (1989) *More heat than light: economics as social physics, physics as nature's economics*. Cambridge University Press, New York.

MISES L. VON (1933) *Grundprobleme der Nationaloekonomie*. Tr. ingl. (1976), *Epistemological problems of economics*. New York University Press, New York.

MISES L. VON (1959) *L'azione umana*. UTET, Turin.

MONTAGUE P. R. (2007) "Neuroeconomics, a view from neuroscience". In *Functional neurology*, 22 (4), pp. 219–234.

MORIN E. (1989) *La conoscenza della conoscenza*. Feltrinelli, Milan.

MORIN E. (1991) "Razionalità e complessità". In *Enciclopedia multimediale delle scienze filosofiche*, Naples.

MORIN E. (2005) *Etica*. Raffaello Cortina Editore, Milan.

MORINI S. (2003) "Prefazione all'edizione italiana". In Gigerenzer G., *Quando i numeri ingannano*. Raffaele Cortina Editore, Milan.

MOTTERLINI M., PIATTELLI PALMARINI M. (2005, eds.) *Critica della ragione economica. Tre saggi: Kahneman, McFadden, Smith*. Il Saggiatore, Milan.

NADER K. (2003) "Memory traces unbound". In *Trends in neurosciences*, 26 (2), pp. 65–72.

NEUMANN J. VON, MORGENSTERN O. (1944) *Theory of games and economic behavior*. Princeton University Press, Princeton, NJ.

NOWAK M. A., PAGE K. M., SIGMUND K. (2000) "Fairness versus reason in the ultimatum game". In *Science*, 289 (5485), pp. 1773–1775.

NOZICK R. (1985) "Newcomb's problem and two principles of choice". In Campbell R. & Sowden L., (eds.), *Paradoxes of rationality and cooperation*. University of British Columbia Press, Vancouver, pp. 114–146.

NOZICK R. (1993) *The nature of rationality*. Princeton University Press, Princeton, NJ.

NUSSBAUM M. C. (2004) *L'intelligenza delle emozioni*. Il Mulino, Bologna.

OATLEY K. (2007) *Breve storia delle emozioni*. Il Mulino, Bologna.

OLIVERIO A. (1998) *L'arte di ricordare*. Rizzoli, Milan.

OLIVERIO A. (1999) *Esplorare la mente. Il cervello tra filosofia e biologia*. Raffaello Cortina, Milan.

OLIVERIO A. (2008) *Geografie della mente. Territori cerebrali e comportamenti umani*. Raffaello Cortina, Milan.

O'DOHERTY J. P. (2004) "Reward representations and reward-related learning in the human brain: insights from neuroimaging". In *Current opinion neurobiology*, 14, pp. 769–776.

OPPENHEIMER D. M. (2003) "Not so fast! (and not so frugal!): rethinking the recognition heuristic". In *Cognition*, 90 (1), pp. B1–B9.

PADOA-SCHIOPPA C., CHIANG-SHAN R. L., BIZZI E. (2005) "Neuronal activity in the supplementary motor area of monkeys adapting to a new dynamic environment". In *Journal of neurophysiology*, 91, pp. 449–473.

PALLER K. A. (2001) "Neurocognitive foundations of human memory". In Medin D. L. (2001, Ed.), *The psychology of learning and motivation*, 40, pp. 121–145. Academic Press, San Diego, CA.

PARFIT D. (1989) *Ragioni e persone*. Il Saggiatore, Milan.

PASCAL B. (1910) *Thoughts* in *Blaise Pascal*, The Harvard Classics, Edited by Charles W. Eliot. Trans. W. F. Trotter. P. F. Collier & Son, New York.

PAYNE J. W., BETTMAN J. R., JOHNSON E. J. (1992) "Behavioral decision research: a constructive process perspective". In *Annual review of psychology*, 43, pp. 87–131.

PAYNE J. W., BETTMAN J. R., JOHNSON E. J. (1993) *The adaptive decision maker*. Cambridge University Press, Cambridge.

PIATTELLI PALMARINI M. (1993) *L'illusione di sapere*. Mondadori, Milan.

PIATTELLI PALMARINI M. (2005) *Psicologia ed economia delle scelte: quattro lezioni al Collège de France*. Codice, Turin.

PIERSON P. (1993) "When effect becomes cause: policy feedback and political change". In *World politics*, 45, pp. 595–628.

PIEVANI T. (2005) *Introduzione alla filosofia della biologia*. Laterza, Rome-Bari.

PINKER S. (1997) *How the mind works*. W. W. Norton & Company, New York. Tr. It. (2000), *Come funziona la mente*. Mondadori, Milan.

POLANYI M. (1951) *The logic of liberty*. Tr. It. (2002) *La logica della libertà*. Rubbettino, Soveria-Mannelli.

POPPER K. R. (1963) *Conjectures and refutations; the growth of scientific knowledge*. Harper & Row, New York.

RAPOPORT A., CHAMMAH A. M. (1965) *Prisoner's dilemma.* University of Michigan Press, Ann Arbor, MI.

RAWLS J. (1971) *A theory of justice.* The Belknap Press of Harvard University Press, Boston.

RAWLS J. (2004) *Lezioni di storia della filosofia morale.* Feltrinelli, Milan.

RECCHIA LUCIANI A. (2007) "Biologia della coscienza". In Maldonato M. (ed), *La coscienza: come la biologia inventa la cultura.* Guida, Naples, 137–238.

RECCHIA LUCIANI A. (2008) "Neuroscienze cognitive e processi decisionali". In Maldonato M. (ed), *Psicologia della decisione.* Ellissi, Naples, pp. 11–68.

REED S. K. (1994) *Psicologia cognitiva.* Il Mulino, Bologna.

REDELMEIER D., KAHNEMAN D. (1996) "Patients' memories of painful medical treatments: real-time and retrospective evaluations of two minimally invasive procedures". In *Pain*, 66, pp. 3–8.

RESNIK D. B. (2003) "Is the precautionary principle unscientific?". In *Studies in history and philosophy of biological and biomedical sciences*, 34, pp. 329–344.

RIBOT T. (1911) *The psychology of the emotions.* Walter Scott Publishing Company, London.

RIEMSCHNEIDER M. (1997) *La religione dei celti. Una concezione del mondo.* Rusconi, Milan.

RILLING J. K., GUTMAN D. A., ZEH T. R., PAGNONI G., BERNS G. S., KILTS C. D. (2002) "A neural basis for social cooperation". In *Neuron*, 35, pp. 395–405.

RIZZELLO S. (1995) "La path-dependency nella teoria economica e il contributo di F. Momigliano". In *Storia del pensiero economico*, 30, pp. 23–52.

RIZZELLO S. (1997) *L'economia della mente.* Laterza, Rome-Bari.

RIZZOLATTI G., SINIGAGLIA C. (2008) *Mirrors in the brain: how our minds share actions, emotions, and experience.* Oxford University Press, Oxford.

ROBBINS L. (1935) *An essay on the nature and significance of economic science.* MacMillan, London.

RUMIATI R., BONINI N. (1992) "Psicologia della decisione e decisioni economiche". In *Sistemi intelligenti*, 4 (3), pp. 357–377.

SABBATUCCI D. (1988) *La religione di roma antica, dal calendario festivo all'ordine cosmico.* Il Saggiatore, Milan.

SAFIRE W. (2003) "The risk that failed". In *The New York Times*, July 10, p. A23.

SAMUELSON P. A. (1977) "St Petersburg paradoxes: defanged, dissected and historically described". In *Journal of economic literature*, 15, pp. 24–55.

SARA S., PRZYBYSLAWSKI J. (1997) "Reconsolidation of memory after its reactivation". In *Behavioural brain research*, 84 (1–2), pp. 241–246.

SARGENT T. J. (1993) *Bounded rationality in macroeconomics: the Arne Ryde memorial lectures.* Clarendon Press, Oxford.

SAVAGE L. J. (1954) *The foundations of statistics.* John Wiley and Sons, New York.

SCHKADE D., PAYNE J. (1994) "How people respond to contingent valuation questions: a verbal protocol analysis of willingness to pay for an environmental regulation". In *Journal of environmental economics and management*, 26, pp. 88–109.

SCHWARTZ B. (2007) "Quando le parole decidono". In *Mente e cervello*, 36, 5, pp. 56–63.

SELIGMAN M. E. P. (2003) *La costruzione della felicità. Che cos'è l'ottimismo, perché può migliorare la vita*. Sperling & Kupfer, Milan.

SELIGMAN M. E. P., CSIKSZENTMIHALYI M. (2000) "Positive psychology: an introduction". In *American psychologist*, 55 (1), pp. 5–14.

SELTEN R. (1991) "Evolution, learning and economic behavior". In *Games and economic behavior*, 3, pp. 3–24.

SELTEN R. (1998) "Aspiration adaptation theory". In *Journal of mathematical psychology*, 42, pp. 191–214.

SELTEN R. (2001) "What is bounded rationality?" In Gigerenzer G., Selten R. (eds.), *Bounded rationality*. The MIT Press, Cambridge, MA, pp. 147–171.

SELTEN R., SELTEN B. (1988) *Models of strategic rationality*. Springer, Berlin.

SHACKLE G. L. S. (1955) *Uncertainty in economics and other reflections*. Cambridge University Press, Cambridge.

SHAPLEY L. S. (1977) "The St Petersburg Paradox: a con game". In *Journal of economic theory*, 10, pp. 439–42.

SHEFRIN H. (2000) *Beyond greed and fear: understanding behavioral finance and the psychology of investment*. Oxford University Press, USA.

SHEFRIN H., THALER R. H. (1992) *Mental accounting, saving, and self-control*. In Lowenstein G., Elster J. (eds.), *Choice over time*. Russell Sage Foundation, New York, pp. 287–330.

SHIVA B., LOEWENSTEIN G., BECHARA A. (2005) "The dark side of emotion in decision-making: when individuals with decreased emotional reactions make more advantageous decisions". In *Cognitive brain research*, 23 (1), pp. 85–92.

SIMON H. A. (1956) "Rational choice and the structure of the environment". In *Psychological review*, 63, pp. 129–138.

SIMON H. A. (1957) *Models of man: social and rational*. Wiley, New York.

SIMON H. A. (1972) "Theories of bounded rationality". In MacGuire C. B., Radner C. (1972) *Decision and organization*. North-Holland, Amsterdam.

SIMON H. A. (1978) "Rationality as process and product of thought". In *American economic review*, 68 (2), pp. 1–16.

SIMON H. A. (1979) "Rational decision making in business organizations" (Nobel Lecture, Stockholm, 1978). In *American economic review*, 69, pp. 493–512.

SIMON H. A. (1985) *Causalità, razionalità, organizzazione*. Il Mulino, Bologna.

SIMON H. A. (1987) "Satisficing". In Eatwell J., Milgate M., Newman P. (eds.), *The new pelgrave: a dictionary of economics*. Macmillan, London, vol. 4, pp. 243–245.

SIMON H. A. (1988) *La ragione nelle vicende umane*. Il Mulino, Bologna.

SIMON H. A. (1990) "Invariants of human behavior". In *Annual review of psychology*, 41, pp. 1–19.

SINGER R., SEYMOUR B., O'DOHERTY J., STEPHAN K. E., DOLAN R. J., FRITH C. D. (2006) "Empathic neural responses are modulated by the perceived fairness of others". In *Nature*, 439, pp. 466–469.

SINGER T., FEHR E. (2005) "The neuroeconomics of mind reading and empathy". In *American economic review*, 95 (2), pp. 340–345.

SLOVIC P. (1972) "Psychological study of human judgment: implications for investment decision making". In *The Journal of finance*, 27 (4), pp. 779–799.

SLOVIC P., FINUCANE M., PETERS E., MACGREGOR D. G. (2002) "The affect heuristic". In Gilovich T. D., Griffin D. W., Kahneman D., (eds.), *Heuristics and biases*. Cambridge University Press, Cambridge, pp. 397–420.

SMITH A. (1776) *An inquiry into the causes of the wealth of nations*. Edinburgh. Tr. It. (1996), *La ricchezza delle nazioni*. UTET, Turin.

SMITH V. L. (2005) "Razionalità costruttivista e razionalità ecologica". In Motterlini M., Piattelli Palmarini M., (eds.), *Critica della ragione economica. Tre saggi: Kahneman, McFadden, Smith*. Il Saggiatore, Milan, pp. 141–220.

SONNEMANS J., SCHRAM A., OFFERMAN T. (1994) "Public good provision and public bad prevention: the effect of framing". In *Working paper*, University of Amsterdam, Roetersstraat; reprinted (1998), *Journal of economic behavior & organization*, 34 (1), pp. 143–161.

SPINOZA B. (2008) *Etica*. Armando, Roma.

SQUIRE L. R. (2007) "Memory systems: a biological concept". In Roediger R., Dudai Y., and Fitzpatrick S. (eds.), *Science of memory: concepts*. Oxford University Press, Oxford, pp. 339–343.

STUTZER A., FREY B. S. (2006) *Economia e felicità. Come l'economia e le istituzioni influenzano il benessere*. Il Sole 24 Ore edizioni, Milan.

SUN TZU (1988) *The art of war*. Cleary T. (trans.), Shambhala, Boston & Shaftesbury, Shambala Publications Editions, Inc, Boston. Tr. It. (1990) *L'arte della Guerra*. Casa Editrice Astrolabio-Ubaldini Editore, Rome.

SUTTON J. (1991) *Sunk costs and market structure*. The MIT Press, Cambridge, MA.

SZEKELY G. J. (1986) *Paradoxes in probability theory and mathematical statistics*. Reidel Publishing Company, Dordrecht.

TABIBNIA G., LIEBERMAN M. D. (2007) "Fairness and cooperation are rewarding: evidence from social cognitive neuroscience". In *Annals of the New York Academy of Sciences*, 1118, pp. 90–101.

THALER R. H. (1980) "Towards a positive theory of consumer choice". In *Journal of economic behavior and organization*, 1, pp. 39–60.

THALER R. H. (1985) "Mental accounting and consumer choice". In *Marketing science*, 4, pp. 199–214.

THALER R. H. (1990) "Saving, fungibility and mental accounts". In *Journal of economic perspectives* 4, pp. 193–205.

THALER R. H. (1991) *Quasi-rational economics*. Russell Sage Foundation, New York.

THALER R. H., JOHNSON E. (1990) "Gambling with the house money and trying to break even: the effects of prior outcomes on risky choice". In *Management science*, 36, pp. 643–660.

TOOBY J., COSMIDES L. (1992) "The psychological foundations of culture". In Barkov J., Cosmides L., Tooby J. (1992, eds.), *The adapted mind: evolutionary psychology and the generation of culture*. Oxford University Press, New York.

TREVI M. (1993) *Saggi di critica neojunghiana*. Feltrinelli, Milan.

TRYPHON A., VONECHE J. H., HOVE J. (1996) *Piaget–Vygotsky: the social genesis of thought*. Psychology Press, Taylor & Francis, Erlbaum (UK). Tr. It. (1998), *Piaget-Vygotskij. La genesi sociale del pensiero*. Giunti, Florence.

TVERSKY A. (2004) *Preference, belief, and similarity: selected writings*. E. Shafir (ed.), MIT Press, Cambridge, MA.

TVERSKY A., KAHNEMAN D. (1971) "Belief in the law of small numbers". In *Psychological bulletin*, 76, pp. 105–110.

TVERSKY A., KAHNEMAN D. (1973) "Availability: a heuristic for judging frequency and probability". In *Cognitive psychology*, 5, pp. 207–232.

TVERSKY A., KAHNEMAN D. (1974) "Judgment under uncertainty: heuristics and biases". In *Science*, 185 (4157), pp. 1124–1131.

TVERSKY A., KAHNEMAN D. (1981) "The framing of decisions and the psychology of choice". In *Science*, 211 (4481), pp. 453–458.

TVERSKY A., SATTAH S., SLOVIC P. (1988) "Contingent weighting in judgment and choice". In *Psychological review*, 95, pp. 371–384.

VAN'T WOUT M., KAHN R. S., SANFEY A. G., ALEMAN A. (2006) "Affective state and decision-making in the ultimatum game". In *Experimental brain research*, 169 (4), pp. 564–568.

VIALE R. (2005) "Quale mente per l'economia cognitiva". In Viale R. (ed.), *Le nuove economie. Dall'economia evolutiva a quella cognitiva: oltre i fallimenti della teoria neoclassica*. Il Sole 24 Ore edizioni, Milan, pp. 20–22.

VULPIANI A. (1994) *Determinismo e caos*. Nuova Italia Scientifica, Rome.

WALD A. (1950) *Statistical decision functions*. John Wiley and Sons, New York.

WALRAS L. (1874) *Elements of pure economics: or the theory of social wealth*. Jaffe W., George Allen and Unwin, London.

WILSON E. O. (1979) *Sociobiologia. La nuova sintesi*. Zanichelli, Bologna.

WILSON J. Q. (1993) *The moral sense*. Free Press, New York.

XIAO E., HOUSER D. (2005) "Emotion expression in human punishment behaviour". In *Procedings of the national academy of sciences of America*, 102 (20), pp. 7398–7401.

XIAO J., PADOA-SCHIOPPA C., BIZZI, E. (2005) "Neuronal correlates of movement dynamics in the dorsal and ventral premotor area in the monkey". In *Experimental brain research*, 168 (1–2), pp. 106–119.

YAMAMOTO T. (2002) *Hagakure. Il libro segreto dei samurai*. Mondadori, Milan.

ZAK P. J. (2004) "Neuroeconomics". In *Philosophical transactions of the royal society biology*, 359, pp. 1737–1748.

# Index

reasoning *(continued)*
  heuristics and biases program, 14, 16
  inductive, 14, 15
  intuition, 47
  mental logic theory, 14–15
  mental models theory, 14, 15–16
  probabilistic, 14, 16
Recchia Luciani, A., 64
reciprocal altruism, 78
recognition heuristics, 28, 29–30, 55–6
Redelmeier, D., 96
Reder, M.W., 39
relational competition, perception of
  happiness, 91
Renaissance philosophers, 8
representativity heuristic, 28
Resnik, D.B., 18
retrograde amnesia, 93, 95
Ribot, T., 52
Ricardo, D., 13
Riemschneider, M., 84
risk
  decision-making, 17–21
  function of utility, 38–9
  normative theories, 48–9
  perceptions of, 4
  and uncertainty, 18
  variable objectives, 34
risk-taking test, 61–2
Ritov, D., 30
Rizzolatti, G., 75
Robbins, L., 13
rules of conclusion, 22–3
rules of decision making, 7
rules of termination, 7
Rumiati, R., 44

Sabbatucci, D., 84
Safire, W., 70
Samuelson, P.A., 12
Sara, S., 95
Sargent, T.J., 37
satisfaction, 32–6, 43–4
  perception of happiness, 90, 91
satisfaction treadmill effect, 90
satisficing heuristics, 29, 36
Sattah, S., 49
Savage, L.J., 19
Schkade, D., 27
Scholastic philosophers, 8
Schram, A., 50
Schwarz, N., 91, 97, 98
science, 8
sciences of nature, 9
search, theory of, 44
searching rules, 7

self-interest, 12, 68, 69, 78
Seligman, M.E.P., 89, 92
Selten, B., 32
Selten, R.
  aspiration adaptation, 32, 33–4
  bounded rationality, 32, 34, 44
  modern economic theory, 36
  Nobel prize for economics, 39
  optimization, 23
  robot basketball task, 31–2
senses, Cartesian dualism, 9
sensory memory, 75
serotonin, 75
Servan-Schreiber, E., 59
Shackle, G.L.S., 18
Shapley, L.S., 12
Shefrin, H., 28, 50
Simon, H., 55
  adaptive decision making, 46
  bounded rationality, 4, 43–4
  cognitive economy, 66
  cognitive limitations, 38, 44
  emotions, 30
  environmental dimension, 37, 38, 44
  errors in reasoning, 27
  existence of constraints, 35, 37
  heuristics, 38
  *homo economicus*, 36
  limits of optimization, 45
  neo-classical economic theory, 43
  normative rationality, 3–4
  Olympic rationality, 36, 42
  satisfaction process, 33, 35, 43–4
  search for alternatives, 22
Singer, T., 63, 68
situational treadmill effect, 90, 91
skin conductance response (S.C.R.), 61, 62
Slovic, P., 16, 30, 49
Smith, A., 12–13
Smith, V.L., 41, 69
somatic markers, 54, 59, 60–1, 74
Sonino, M., 16
Sonnemans, J., 50
Spelke, E., 72
Spinoza, B., 11, 52–3
spontaneous order, 40, 41
sporting competition, 83–4
Squire, L.R., 95
statistical data, 5–6
statistical tools, 35
Stephenson, G.M., 83
stereotypes, 28
strategic interaction, 39
Stroebe, W., 83
Stutzer, A., 99
subjective value, 12